GIVE THE
PERFECT GIFT

TO THE TEEN IN YOUR LIFE

Canvas is a wonderful way to
encourage teen writers and artists.

Order our issues on amazon or visit
www.canvasliteraryjournal.com/previous-issues

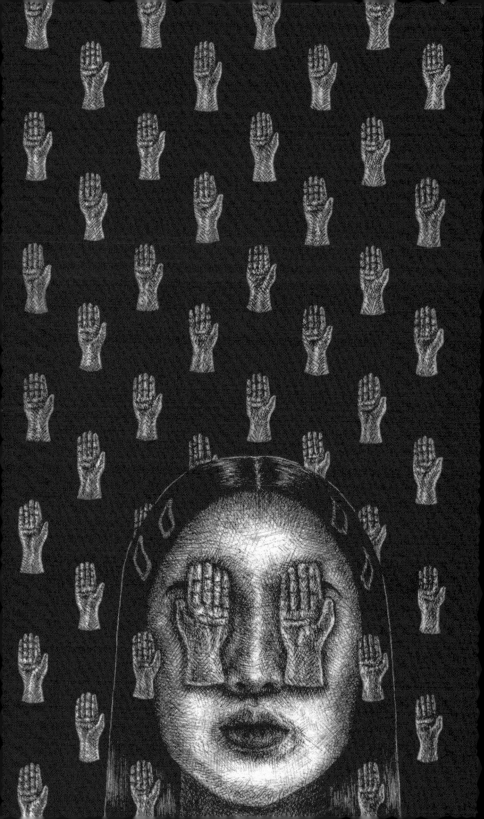

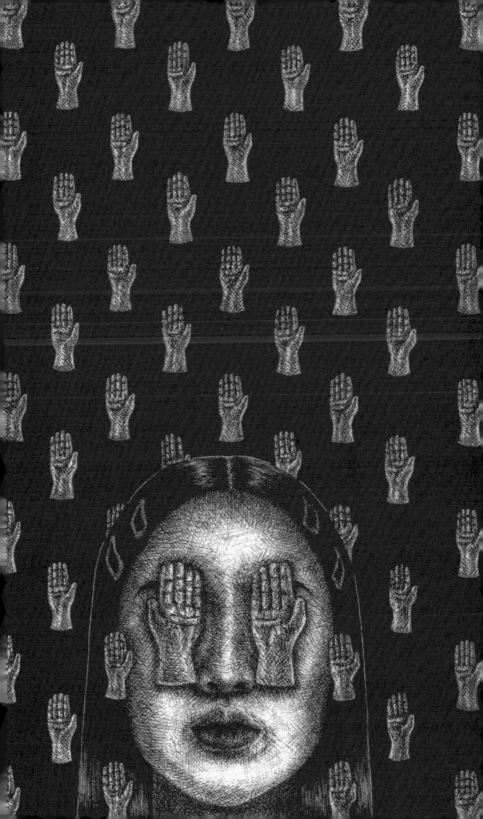

CANVAS

TEEN LITERARY JOURNAL

Previous Issues

SUMMER 2019. Vol. 21

SPRING 2019. Vol. 20

WINTER 2019, Vol. 19

AUTUMN 2018, Vol. 18

SPRING 2017, Vol. 17

WINTER 2017, Vol. 16

AUTUMN 2016, Vol. 15

SUMMER 2016, Vol. 14

SPRING 2016, Vol. 13

WINTER 2016, Vol. 12

AUTUMN 2015, Vol. 11

SUMMER 2015, Vol. 10

SPRING 2015, Vol. 9

WINTER 2015, Vol. 8

AUTUMN 2014, Vol. 7

SUMMER 2014, Vol. 6

SPRING 2014, Vol. 5

WINTER 2014, Vol. 4

AUTUMN 2013, Vol. 3

SUMMER 2013, Vol. 2

SPRING 2013, Vol. 1

TEEN LITERARY JOURNAL

AUTUMN 2019

VOLUME 22

OUR THANKS

We would like to sincerely thank all the teen board members who gave their blood, sweat, and tears to *Canvas* since our first issue in Spring 2013.
You are all fine editors and fine people.

Ana Anaya
Abby Johnson
Sophie Moon
Sarah Moore
Marcelo Ortiz
Delaney Palma
Julia Taylor
Sophia Trzcinski
Bella Watts
Amelia Willard
Tori Wilson
Peter Wood
Ali Wrona
Cheyenne Zaremba
Vanessa Zimmerman
Lisa Zou

And the adult advisors and Writers & Books staff who helped *Canvas* grow and flourish:

Sally Bittner Bonn
Lindsey Buck
Chris Fanning
Joe Flaherty
Daniel Herd
Kristen King

Masthead

TEEN EDITORIAL BOARD
(Autumn 2019)

Abby Asmuth
Yasmine Chokrane
Leo Cox
Evie de Rubertis
Aditi Jain
Haripriya Jalluri
Jessica Jiang
Anushka Karthik
Ann Kennedy
Aria Khalique
Christian Kim
Andrea Liao
Po-Ting Lin (Duke)
Francesca Mirthil
Julia Pelletier
Tula Singer
Muneebah Umar
Lea Wang-Tomic
Manya Zhao

ADULT STAFF

EDITOR-IN-CHIEF
Lindsay Herko

PUBLISHER
Nina Alvarez

PROOFREADER
Linnea Schaefer

Canvas Teen Literary Journal publishes the work of teen writers and artists 13-18 years old, read and rated by a board of teen editors. Publisher Nina Alvarez and Editor-in-Chief Lindsay Herko oversee the publication of the journal.

Visit *Canvas* at CanvasLiteraryJournal.com to read the online journal.

Issues are also available for sale in paperback through amazon, or by loan from a growing number of libraries.

For more information, contact canvaslitboard@gmail.com

Cover art "Camouflage" by Hyung Jin Lee
Frontispiece "Volunteer" by Sydney Lee

Cover design and print layout by Nina Alvarez
Canvas logo by Ali Wrona

ISBN-9781695239609

CONTENTS

HALLOWEEN

FOX - JAW

Olivia Bell

i. you live in that cadent interlude, a valley scooped from between the mountains, a layer of alpenglow smothering the peaks.

ii. winter is the natural state of things here. there's something useless about summer, like a fawn stumbling over itself as it learns to walk, then relearns it every season. slender legs flecked with white, slender legs shaking.

iii. sometimes summer's wide, hot breath murmurs its way over the cusp of fall, and the leaves are molting but the air is still brightening and then you feel like crying even though rust-colored september means you no harm. it's as if she's mumbling to you, with her withering voice, "look, here's a newness and a dying all at once."

iv. in the heart's useless bright stoa, your face glows, warmer than a caldarium, a sunbeam through the oculus of my heart, and the light outside is a bacchanalia, like my melting gaze, and suddenly i want to fall at your feet and kiss them and kiss them and

v. may the time come when our hearts meet, perhaps in some dreamland beyond the strands and mountains. my sleeper in the valley. my light, my life, my garden, my rib.

vi. summer comes to a restless close at the quiet peak of an inhalation. and i know this is the order of things but there is still something unsparing about the way winter moves in. like fox-jaw, sly, elegant, comely. as if she's saying, "look, there are no scavengers here. my teeth are bloodied, but only with the brutal verdancy of this season's repeated acquiescence to endings."

WHAT DOES ONE DO WHEN THEY MEET A GOD?

ALIZA LI

He found me in the summer.

He found me lounging in a grassy meadow in Amyclae, a crown of peonies nestled in my hair. Lying in the sun, I felt the coolness of a shadow across my face and looked up to see him standing above me.

I watched the flex and pull of *taut muscles,* of the solid bronze pillars of his arms, and felt heat pool into the pit of my stomach. His smile, a pale and shiny moon, entranced me immediately.

Like a fool, I did not know who he was until he spoke. He was a stranger, a probability, a summer tryst. Beguiling and magnetic but deniable. I twisted a lock of hair between my fingers and wondered how his arm would look curled around my waist, reassured by the power I held to withhold myself from him.

Then, he spoke and I knew.

The soft thunder of his voice reverberated through my ears and into my skull. He spoke with an intonation that both caressed me like a gentle breeze and choked the breath out of my lungs.

For a split second, I remembered my mother. When I was young, she would tell me the stories of the gods, of charming men who stole away innocent children, of the glorious god Apollo. God of the sun. God of warm bodies and soft touch. God who wove verse together, string over string, and tied me a knotted veil to cover my eyes.

Was there ever anything I could keep from you?

He pushed me delicately into the grass and entered me softly and slowly, like a finger dips into the flesh of a clam and encircles the pearl within.

The pink of his skin kissed mine, and his heat became my heat and my heat became his.

He sang a melody into the dip of my collarbone, let the notes echo in my ribs.

I giggled as the thin scruff of his beard tickled my bare chest. As he pushed in and stole the warmth from my lungs, I remembered my mother and the stories of the gods. I remembered her warnings. I lost myself in the heat of Apollo's gaze and the caress of his mouth.

Will you ever leave?

I was fine at first. I fell asleep on his chest and woke up in the grass, alone. I let out a sigh of relief and ignored the ache in my bones. *Good*, I thought, *it is good to be only a preoccupation and nothing more.*

Even I could not lie to myself.

For weeks, I returned to the meadow. *The flowers were especially beautiful there*, I told myself, *my mother would love these peonies, sunshine is good for the health*. I returned again and again. For weeks, the only footprints in the grass were my own.

It is strange how someone can leave and return so silently, as if they were never gone. Apollo found me bathing in the river, an innocent smile across his face betrayed by the glint of hunger in his eyes. His eyebrows furrowed with thought as his gaze drifted from my flushed cheeks to my shoulders to my chest and down below.

I held my arms out like the wings of a swan and invited him in. He drank in my smile, gorged on my breath, got fat on my blood. Then he settled back, pliant and relaxed, and gently stroked my shivering, skinny arm.

"I love you," I whispered, rubbing the skin between the bumps of my ribs. Apollo smiled.

Will I see you again?

In autumn, we celebrated my birthday. Apollo asked me what I wanted for a gift. *Moons? Stars? The world?*

I laughed. *Flowers, my lord. Just flowers.*

He settled a plot of wilderness and filled it with thousands of peonies, daisies, roses, lilies, all for me. For the first time (and not the last), as I looked out into the vast meadow he created, I was afraid of him. Afraid of the power he held that only a wave of his hand could fell mountains and dry up rivers. And afraid of the fact that a powerful being such as him would submit the will of someone like me. My mother had sensed for a while that something was wrong. I left home for too long and came back too flushed in the face. She made a habit of inspecting my neck and legs when I returned. I didn't let her know that the marks were there, only invisible.

She sighed a lot more and held my younger sisters closer to her chest. I almost felt sorry for not telling her. But then I returned to Apollo, and for a few hours, I forgot everything about her and about myself, even my own name.

Will you remember me?

For three months, I didn't see him. I paid no attention to it at first. Sometimes gods did that. Sometimes they leave and don't return for a while and come back as if no time had passed at all. I understood the needs of the immortal, to fluctuate between one plane of existence and another.

Besides, the meadow he gifted me felt like a promise. We had solidified a pact between us. I sat in the meadow and held my love for him close to my chest like a prayer.

Three months in, I visited the marketplace by Sparta in search of a new hairbrush for my youngest sister. Browsing the stalls and vendors, I suddenly remembered his temple was there. *I'll stop by for a visit,* I thought to myself. Give an offering so he knows I'm still thinking about him. Maybe... just maybe, it'll remind him to come back.

Somehow, I knew he was there as soon as my sandaled foot touched the marble steps. I almost ran up to greet him, but a thought stopped me. *He's not at Olympus,* I realized. He's here, but he hasn't come to visit.

Dread is a slow trickle. It starts in the bottom of the stomach like most feelings do and spreads up the torso to the heart. It always begins slowly and then comes all at once, a torrent of shame and fear.

I crept up the stairs, gripping the front of my chiton in clenched hands. I heard his voice, soft yet thunderous, joined by another, light and feminine. A woman.

He was with a woman, a priestess of his own temple. She had to have known who he was. She must not have cared, laughing and smiling up at him, caressing his arm. For a sick moment, I wanted to call out and confront him. To play the part of the jealous lover. But I knew my place and crept back slowly from the temple steps and walked all the way back home. It was only when I reached home that I realized I forgot to buy the hairbrush.

Who are you to me?

Apollo found me again. Lying in the meadow he gifted me, I heard his voice call out

to me from above. He smiled down from his flaming chariot, a reflection of the sun itself as he greeted my prone figure with a lazy wave. He had the look of a man confident in himself and the ruse he disguised behind a grin.

Like a shedding viper, I imagined peeling away the layers of his immortality from his body, dimming the glossy tint that enveloped him. I imagined turning him human and laying bare all his shame.

I played my part well. A young and naive lover, dutifully awaiting their beloved. We each had our parts to play. He pretended to love me, and I pretended it was true.

Now, I wonder if he knew at the time what I learned of him. Perhaps he didn't care that I knew. For some reason that sickens me more.

I understand how people fall apart. We let a feeling sit in our brain for months, growing and festering like a bloody sore, like a disease, until it consumes our entire body. I didn't eat for days. I shed the fat around my chin and under my eyes until my skin turned a sallow pallor. I slept for only a few hours each night and always in the meadow. I let him take me over and over and didn't return to my home for weeks.

My mother screamed at me when she saw me. I wonder how I looked in her eyes, her child reduced to a skeletal figure. My sisters hid between her legs and avoided my gaze. She threw my clothes at me and locked the door behind her. I didn't bother to wait or ask for forgiveness. I simply left.

How does it end?

Sometimes, I wonder if it was truly an accident. He was a

god. He could do anything. A god of archery, his aim always ran true. How could he miss?

I ran my hand along the smooth edge of the discus and felt the cool stone beneath my fingertips. Several paces behind me, Apollo stood with a discus of his own in his outstretched hand. His form was perfect. I heard the quiet swoop of stone flying and turned around to look. The last thing I saw was his smiling face. They built a temple for me in Amyclae. My mother never visits but sometimes my sisters sneak away to look at the ceremonies they hold in my honor.

Apollo left something for me, a last parting gift. A flower, delicate and pure, the one the Greeks call the most beautiful of all flowers.

Hyacinth. Beautiful, tragic Hyacinth.

LOVING

SOPHIA HLAVATY

i. origin
they're out there, those particles that determine life's natural laws. in chemistry, we learned about the second law of thermodynamics; how, left alone, life will always become less structured; how we are led to a gradual descent into disorder. i was taught to be wary. God watches you when you watch the television, when you eat dinner, when you sleep at night. say your prayers; beg for forgiveness for the misery your existence caused your parents or no more orange candy, no more toys, no more school. but i guess it was all a fairytale. everything has been predestined for us. we are mortals: we fall apart in the end.

****

leviathan (episode one)
Marina, they called her. Marina, Marina, from the sea, the most beautiful child. "Marina, where is your home?" "the sea, the sea." when they baptized her, the priest said that her spirit would hunt for water. the ceremony was long, and the heat made my thoughts plod through my consciousness as if there were sandbags attached to each period. i turned my head to the cool breeze coming from the window, and stared at the sequence of innumerable clouds strewn across the sky. here and there in the distance, the sun's golden fingers stitched an artificial glow through the green architecture, designing fugitive shadows, concepts, that were previously veiled from achievability. the petals of a nearby flower bush scattered in the breath of the wind. the animals (jellyfish? elephants? dinosaurs?) in the heavens cried balsamic red tears that night, the color so very much like the blood of the chicken whose head my grandmother cut off that same afternoon.

******

ii. dreamsongs

in this church i like to pretend that i'm religious. afternoon sun filters through a stained glass window; wavelengths splinter into fragmentary echoes of colors that hunger to carve spiritual meaning out of light. we cry for mercy together with the priest, whose talk, a permanent, rumbling exhortation, expels a rhythm of sounds and syllables conflated with foreign dreams of latent salvation of which i yearn to understand. the words, soldiers animated from origami paper, emerge like molten liquid and burn the roof of the priest's mouth. they pound like waves through the pews, breaking into tumultuous melodies that disappear and drown in our vacillation between exacting our idealized visions or accepting our guilty subordination to our sins. yet as the service continues, the moonlight elucidates the design of their countenances built upon the determination that *tomorrow will be better, tomorrow i will be good.* in this moment of ephemeral satisfaction, the ostinatos of forgiveness and kindness provide a violent intoxication that awakens in me the presence of hidden, unknown, invisible realities governed by a hope that is inherently ineffable. the contours of my soul change as they are offered narcotic refreshment by the church's soma: comfort. "body and blood for you, body and blood for you." "not for her; she hasn't been reborn." "mother of God, pray for us sinners now, and at the hour of our death," we chant. as the days pass, the melodies slip through my fingertips, transfigured into a haunting descending scale in minor key. church becomes a distant memory, a state of being under the custody of a supreme pleasure to which i cannot hope to recollect.

my grandmother keeps a shell on the fireplace mantle. the shell's glossy affectation is marred by its orange spine: a bloodline that contorts and succumbs, nailed to its own cross. when i hold the shell to my ear, i hear the rushing of the ocean. yet despite its immediate accessibility, i am unable to manifest that essential nature of possibility. its spirit is suffocated by the shell itself. the overwhelming sensation of comfort is hidden within the realmof memory; it has made an indelible imprint on my experiences at church of which i claw at to cradle, yet am powerless to access and replicate within the bounds of reality.

******

leviathan (episode two)
dear diary, Marina is an ugly cousin: hair too straight, skin too pale, eyes more like the reedy, muddy creek behind grandfather's house than the roaring great ocean. each morning, she would open a window and look towards the horizon to see if something had changed in the world; hopefully, the universe would be a little wider, a little bolder if it did.

******

iii. inheritance
how many carrots does it take to turn my skin orange? i think this as my mother and i stand in the line for changing rooms. we had free time, and she was the one who suggested we try on dresses at the mall. i take the dresses from her, change, and show her how each looks. she talks loudly about how pretty each one is, and how she can't decide which to purchase; the dresses are far too expensive, and we both know that she is pretending. a salesperson comes over to help us. "wow," he says, "those dresses look beautiful on her." my mother stares at his face when he talks to us, and after she pulls out the picture from her bag. it's a picture of her when she was in high school that she shows to everyone. "look," she says, "i was pretty too. look at me. i was beautiful back then." in the parking lot, she tells me that if i maintain my body i can buy those dresses when i get older. "don't become a size four, sophia, or else you'll be fat," she laughs. "i know," i say. "you've told me before." when we come home, she calls my Dad to see what show He wants to be playing on the television above the kitchen table, what food He wants to

eat, and where He will be sleeping tonight.

******

leviathan (episode three)
eleven years after she was born, our families stuffed our clothes, towels, beach balls, and shovels in the car and traveled to the ocean together for the first time. Marina's mother drove the three hours to cape may, singing gospel music with Marina's dad and Marina. at the beach, we built four sandcastles that each had two pale white shells glistening at the top and encircled the castles with a moat dug one foot deep. "palaces for Marina," they laughed. when dawn came, marina rushed back to the sand. the castles were wiped away; like unidentified corpses, only a suggestion of who they were, the moat dug one foot deep, remained. Marina looked to the ocean, and the ocean howled back. before we drove home, as we washed the sand from our bodies and I removed the broken white shells from my feet, marina stood by the edge of the water and turned her back to the horizon. one day, Marina realized the world was too big for her and now, her window remains closed.

"Marina," I called to her. "Marina, Marina, from the sea. Marina, where is your home?"

NOCTURNE IN THE FIST
OF THE AQUARIUM

Ana Chen

the organ gargles in my dream where
all the men are underwater and a mermaid beheads them
one by one.

we are at a wedding and i am
studying
the apoptosis of vanilla, godiva pearls menstruating
into basement salt.

in these mercurial tides the benthos is glass. leaves
with screen door eyes, teeth hard shards
of the unwanted. my lips are chapped red.

the shrimp and my moods cuddle in
the crevasses of my nails. my hands weather white
but only in the brine of my knuckles.

i consider the concept of one. a head
floats past. broad nose spilling into sandstone jaw: bow tie
bouquet
of so many arteries.

the mermaid swims to me and i try to tell her she is beautiful,
cerulean scars bubbling over her breasts. yes, she tells me, i
know. and
with the tender brush of a mother, she shreds the veins

from my neck.

After the Failed Audition

Jodie Meng

I wait under a streetlight that pools
Lemonade onto concrete and sends
Plumes of mosquitoes to my tender
Skin. The gentrified bakery smells of
Butter and cigarettes. I breathe in
secondhand smoke and listen to
the music of howling dogs and
oblique highways. My heart beats for
four minutes and thirty-three seconds;
I fake synesthesia to fill the space.
Tonight, there are no constellations,
Only sheets of burnt coal and scattered
Pushpins on a map. I wish upon the
Dirt moons under my fingernails.
My ride never comes.

THOUGHTS & PRAYERS

ALI FISHMAN

The moment we lose our innocence is hard to pinpoint. It happens gradually and over time. We only realize that it is gone once it is too late, once the world has ripped away our innocence one event at a time. I tightly grip my pencil as I quickly push out the final details of my history notes. The girl next to me repeatedly taps her pen on the desk. After what feels like an eternity the teacher admits defeat by dismissing class. After the internal, silent celebration I pack up my books, sling my backpack onto my shoulder, and follow my classmates to lunch. Leaving the classroom is like taking a breath of fresh air. I walk through the hallways hearing heated debates about the latest NBA game and excited chatter about the after-school soccer game. I spot my best friend standing by the neon pink peer tutoring posters. I quickly walked over to say hi before sprinting to my next class. Before I could even complain about my upcoming math test, the loudspeaker blares throughout the school announcing our lockdown drill.

A switch flips in the school as the 300 students who were once energetically buzzing with conversation fall silent as they make their way to their lockdown rooms. We march like soldiers prepared for battle. Our bodies fall into a single file line and our mouths don't dare to crack a smile. I quickly and efficiently place myself behind the desk in the library, my assigned position. I sit there dead silent. No speaking, no sudden movements, no standing up. We all know the rules.

The clock counts down the exact fifteen minutes in which the lockdown drill takes place. The second alarm sounds, signaling five minutes left of this routine drill. I then close my eyes and wait for the last alarm to sound signaling the end of the weekly lockdown drill. My head falls into knees as the silence of the library becomes deafening. My mind begins to wander and for the first time I actually think about the 15 minutes I spend in this library every week. Every other week for as long as I could remember a new headline would surface with another horrible mass shooting somewhere in the United States. Leaders would appear on every media outlet sending their thoughts and prayers. Wishing the families of the victims their best. Then life would just continue, nothing would change. More people were killed, more lives were destroyed, no laws were changed. That is the routine our country fell into. These lockdown drills are part of that routine. Instead of changing the pattern of destructive violence that is eating our country alive, the government sends their thoughts and prayers. Thoughts and prayers don't magically fix situations. They don't implement gun control or protect citizens from the multiple violent attacks that seem to happen biweekly. I have to take time out of my day to practice protecting myself from the inevitable event of a shooting. Instead of creating laws that will stop these horrible events from happening, we train to protect ourselves from the inevitable.

My eyes sting as I lift my face out of my knees. This is the moment. This is the moment where I realized my innocence was gone. My innocence was not the belief that bad things never happened. I always knew the world was not perfect. I knew bad things happened. My innocence was the belief that things could get better. That the leaders we put all of our trust in could help solve problems for their citizens, not continue to fight with one another. The final alarm sounds and the school snaps out of its trance. I see smiles return to my classmates faces and conversation begins to fill the halls once again. This is our routine. This is our story. Every week we will have a fifteen minute lockdown drill that prepares elementary school students for something that was once unthinkable. We have to change our story. Thoughts and prayers are not enough. No matter how bad things get we can never relinquish hope that it will get better, because the world has to get better.

ILLUSION

ALEXIS YANG

I try not to remember.

Iowa snow coats the windshield of my rental car. Flakes nestle against the wipers, burrow against the wheels. We never got snow like this in New Jersey. The cascading flakes and spotless road almost look pretty, but then I remember that snow is just crystallized rain, and rain isn't pretty.

A month ago, I asked to visit you at your house over Christmas break. It's been a year since I've seen you. We went to high school together in New Jersey, held hands and promised that when we went to college, we'd tell each other everything. But now we're freshmen. I'm living in a New York City dormitory and you're living in your father's house. No matter how many phone calls we make, it feels like we are hiding the truth about ourselves.

Now here I am, sitting in a broken-down car in central Iowa. Your father is away on business, so we'll have the house to ourselves. I'm telling myself that this will just be an ordinary visit, where we will talk about the classes we are taking and the food we are eating. But there are the doubts again—doubts about what I will say to you, what you will say to me.

The memories keep flooding back. How we used to sneak out on the weekends. The lies we concocted. The alibis we told our parents, all those movie theaters we never went to. Your voice telling me that you were okay, you were fine, everything was fine, everything was fine.

My foot taps against the car floor, rapid-fire. I try to focus on the falling snow. The empty road. A smudge on the windshield. I called you earlier, my phone to my ear and your name,

Madeline Meyer, on the screen. I said my car broke down. You said okay, you were on your way. You called me Eleanor, not Ellie. You never call me Eleanor.

I check my phone. Two bars. It shifts to three, then slips back down again. I want to call a tow truck. I tell myself I don't feel that pit in my stomach, that darkness that comes when I remember our hands together, the curse of being girls.

Last year, we went everywhere together. When I told my parents I would be going on a day trip with friends, I asked if you wanted to take a train to Central Park. Those weekends, we held hands and walked and tossed bread to the pigeons. We sat on benches and you pulled diecast cars from your pockets, watched them glint in the sunlight. I knew your hand better than mine. The creases on your palm, the words I whispered in your ear—

I'm shivering. The door handle is ice-cold. Central Park and diecast cars—that wasn't how it was. And now all our phone calls, all the trivial things you tell me about your greyhound and your school's hockey team, all the trivial things I tell you about my classes—that's not how things are.

I wonder if you remember how I rushed us home from Central Park. I fudged movie tickets and restaurant receipts, false evidence for my time with you. I made sure that my parents never questioned if you were more than a friend.

My fears started with my cousin Carter. When I was eight and he was sixteen, my aunt and uncle found him dead in the bathroom with an empty bottle of painkillers. They didn't know why he did it. The police had an investigation and found texts between my cousin and another boy. Carter said he loved him. He said Carter was a fag.

I remember my parents' conversation, my ear pressed to their closed door. *Carter never told anyone,* they said. *He just let his feelings brew.*

That wasn't the Carter I knew. He brought me to the candy store, played Scrabble with me and let me win. I didn't recognize this swarm of hushed whispers about the incident. I never knew his dark secrets, everything he never told anybody.

By the time I reached high school, my parents never mentioned Carter. His name an unspoken whisper, an untouched subject. But I never forgot. Part of me was still listening with my ear to my parents' door, hearing about how he *couldn't cope* and *held everything in* and *never faced his problems.*

And when I met you and felt my face reddened to my ears,

I slammed the bathroom door shut and watched the ceiling spin above me. I couldn't be like Carter. I couldn't. And then I wondered if Carter felt himself falling and ignored his feelings, kept them from everyone else. Just kept living and telling himself that nothing was wrong.

It's been thirty minutes since I called; you will be here soon. My mind races to think of what to say to you. Questions about college. Grades. Roommates. But all I can think of are the things we never talk about: my feelings, your diecast cars. All the secrets from last year that we tried to escape.

A buzzing sound probes the air, repeats in steady succession. It takes me a moment to realize that it is my phone.

I can see headlights down the road, like a set of alien eyes. Your name forms on the screen: Madeline Meyer. Standard font, no profile picture.

I raise my phone to my ear and try to speak.

"Eleanor?" your voice probes.

I'm staring at the headlights and the snow and the Iowa road. "Eleanor, are you there?"

I blink. Your car is facing mine.

"Yeah," I say. "Yeah, I'm here."

My mind is racing. I'm thinking about what will happen next. I'll open my car door. You'll open yours. I'll see your hair spilling out from under your cap and remember how it used to feel between my fingers.

I hang up the phone, open the door and step out. I strain to see through your windshield. You're wearing a gray cap and a winter coat; I think it's blue. I can see your brown hair. Your nose. Your cheekbones.

And then you're standing in between the headlights and we're facing each other, hands stuffed in pockets. The air's too cold and too clean and too sharp. For a moment, I want you to step forward and offer your hand. I want to take it like we're in Central Park, hold on like we'll never let go, like it's normal.

"You going to say hello?" you say, smiling like it's just a smile, joking like it's just a joke.

It's too quiet. The road is empty save for my car and yours. I can hear snow crunching beneath my boots, see clouds of my breath forming in the air, feel Iowa snow settling around us. Flakes cascade from the sky, white and spotless and perfect. As they coat our hair and shoulders, I wonder if they could cover us completely. Given enough time, maybe they could.

We've been apart for so long. You've existed on my phone and in text messages, and now here you are. Feet are separating us, not miles. But I can't will myself to move.

My mouth tugs into a smile. I don't know if it's real, but I keep it on anyway. I still can't get words out, so I cross the snowy ground between us and put my arms around you. Last time we hugged, we were in your family's house. But now we're a year older. We're halfway across the country and contact is awkward. We don't stay long, but when we draw away, I feel incomplete.

I should tell you that I missed you. I don't know if you want to tell me this too, if it's lingering on your lips. But too much time passes and I say instead, "Yeah, so I got bad luck with the car and everything."

"It's only a rental," you reply. "You can get it towed."

I nod. I'm supposed to respond, but too much time passes. You breathe in and smile and act as if it's not awkward. "Come on," you suggest. "I'll drive you to my house."

When I slide into the passenger's side, your car smells like peppermint. Fake peppermint.

You turn the key. The engine rumbles alive.

An air freshener shaped like a pine tree hangs from the rear-view mirror.

Peppermint.

"Since when do you like air fresheners?" I ask.

"I don't know," you reply, giving me a lopsided smile.

You think I'm joking.

I gaze out at the road ahead. I should ask how you're doing.

Last year, you pretended to be okay. In the heat of June, you wore sweatshirts to hide your arms. When classmates asked you why you wore them, you said it was comfortable. When they asked me the real reason why, I said it was nothing.

You were the girl who wore jeans year-round and never put

her hair up, who kept toy cars in her locker and didn't change for gym class. You gave yourself names: Avid Collector, Jeans Enthusiast, Creature of Habit. You told yourself that nobody would question.

You were covering up. I know it now, as we sit in the same car on the same road. You were covering up your father's business suits, the way he smiled and said good morning. Because beneath the façade were the bruises he gave you. Your tears in the bathroom. His voice echoing inside you, eating away at the marrow of your bones. And you tried to hide everything with sweatshirts "for comfort," scarves "for fashion," long sleeves because your arms were "too thin." All to hide the scars beneath.

I feel my chest tighten. "How are you doing, Madeline?"

Your eyes are fixed on the road. My watch ticks softly. "I'm doing fine," you respond. "College is good."

The façade, the façade.

"Okay," I reply. "College is good for me too."

This time you glance at me. "You meet some nice people?"

I feel my fingers drum against the seat. "Yeah, I guess," I mumble, and stare at a fallen tree outside the window.

Maybe you think this visit will just be a hello. A how-are-you. But I'm thinking about your diecast cars, that old collection your mother left before she died giving birth to you. You used to buy one every week, expanding your collection. I imagined your cars growing life-size. Your hand curling around the door, pulling it open, grasping the steering wheel. Driving away.

Last year, I gave you train rides, Central Park, refuge upon refuge. Here you are in Iowa with the illusion of distance, of being far from New Jersey and New York, and yet you are still living with your father.

You could still have bruises.

You could still be hiding.

You could become like Carter, covering up for the world, telling yourself that you are safe.

I want to stop the car and explain everything right now. I could tell you about Carter, about my ear against my parents' door, about sweatshirts and bruises and toy cars and everything they're doing to you, everything you don't realize. Because if you never know—

"I got it for a dollar," you're saying.

"What?"

"The air freshener. Smells good, doesn't it?"

"Yeah, it smells like peppermint."

"That's because it is," you reply. You say it like it's simple, like it's truth.

I wonder how long we can keep talking about air fresheners and college. We keep filling conversations with meaningless words, building a wall between us and a veil over our faces.

We drive through your town. It's small. We pass the post office and the diner and the general store, all coated in perfect white snow. When we pull into your driveway, you kill the engine and open the door.

Your house is white and boxlike, so it blends into the snow. You unlock the front door and I grab my bag and we walk in.

It isn't much warmer inside than outside. When I kneel to place my bag on the floor, coldness seeps from the tiles. Your greyhound trots toward me, dog tags jangling, and begs for attention.

"I'll heat up some soup," you announce, and motion for me to sit at the table. It's made of synthetic wood that's meant to look real. The greyhound leans against my legs, his body heavy, and I run my fingers along his sleek ears. In front of me, there's a fridge with a magnet shaped like an eggplant. I look at the frayed rug in the living room and the coffee table with a nick in one of its corners. I wonder how it got there.

It doesn't take long for me to realize: your father was here. Your father lives here. He sits on that brown couch, places mugs on that coffee table. Your father, who smiled and said good morning. Your father, who gave you bruises.

I swallow hard.

"Are you cold?" you ask. Suddenly you're standing in front of me with a bowl of tomato soup.

"Uh, no," I lie.

"You're shivering. I'll turn up the heat."

You walk away and I raise soup to my mouth. It trembles in the spoon, or maybe it's my hand wavering. I've had two spoonfuls when I notice the blue diecast car on the shelf in the living room, wedged between books on macroeconomics.

When you return, you ladle soup into a bowl for yourself and sit down next to me.

"Madeline," I blurt.

You pause. My chest aches. I can almost feel my ear against wood, listening to my parents speaking about Carter.

Couldn't cope.

Held everything in.

Never faced his problems.

"Are you still pretending?" I ask.

Your brows draw together. "What do you mean, pretending?"

I can't tell if you know what I mean. Maybe you're just avoiding the question, telling yourself everything's all right.

"Come on," I argue. "Stop saying that. You didn't tell me much after you moved here, and you told me even less after we went to college. Madeline, I brought you to Central Park all those times. Remember that? I brought you there because I thought I could help you. I gave you an escape from him, and now—"

You aren't moving. The greyhound slinks away, but you're sitting still. That's something about you that I forgot: you've always been patient.

"After all he did to you Madeline, you just—you can't act like nothing's wrong."

"I'm not acting like nothing's wrong."

I stand and walk into the living room and grab the diecast car. Beneath my fingers, it feels heavy and slick. It's been so long since I've held one of these. "Do you still collect these cars?" I ask, walking back into the kitchen.

You're standing now, but you don't answer.

"Do you still have that old collection? That one your mother gave you?"

Never had a chance to give. I see the correction rise in your throat, fight its way to your mouth. You force it back down and nod. "Of course I do."

We've gotten so used to silence now, to never questioning each other. But we can't do that anymore. "I never understood why you collect them," I say. "I went along with it, but I . . ."

You shake your head and avert your gaze, pushing your hair behind your ear. "I just... I told you my mother bought a set of cars for me. When I was eight years old, my father told me that she loved to travel. She loved taking road trips by herself in this red Cadillac. But he wanted her to just settle down. Become a mother. He wanted to control her." You take the diecast car and rest it in your palm. Your fingers curl around the grille, swallow the tires. "Then she passed, and he had me. And Eleanor, I'm not . . . I'm not what he wanted. Or my mother wanted."

I open my mouth to object, but you continue with the car clenched tight in your palm. "He noticed me, Eleanor. I tried to keep it a secret that I liked girls, but he suspected for a long time. It was the girl friends I invited over, and how I never wore makeup, and those toy cars—it was always the cars, ever since I was born. When I was fourteen, I put this miniature sports car on my dresser. My father looked at it and said to me, 'Your mother and I wanted a boy.'"

The house is so quiet. The walls and floorboards hum with a deep ache. Your face contorts as you finally put together the puzzle pieces, assembling this picture you've built but never seen before. "My mother always wanted to leave in that Cadillac. I don't believe my father when he says it was just traveling. She wanted to get away from him. She never did, but these cars give me hope that I can."

I step closer to you and my hand gently touches yours. It uncurls, revealing the blue diecast car and the red marks it's left on your palm. "Madeline," I say as I meet your gaze, "toy cars won't take you away from him. You can't escape if you're covering up all the time."

You bite your lip and set the car onto the table.

"You didn't have to go to college here," I tell you. "You didn't have to live with your father. You could have come to New York with me."

"Eleanor," you say evenly, "I couldn't come to New York with you."

"You can still transfer."

You shake your head. Your voice is still level. "Eleanor, do you know why you wanted to visit me?"

Answers throw themselves at me: because I wanted to say hello again. Because I wanted to help you. Because I love you.

"Not because you wanted to help me," you say. "You wanted to come because you're afraid of yourself. You need me to tell you that you're alright."

I don't know what you're talking about. I am alright. I get up and fall asleep at reasonable hours. I don't drink beer like my classmates do. I don't have bruises.

"I am alright," I say.

You draw in your lip, then cross into the living room and return with an economics textbook. The yellowed, water-stained pages are filled with everything random—poems, pressed flowers, clippings from maps.

"Scrapbook?" I ask.

"Yeah, scrapbooking helps me relax." You pause and then add, "My father doesn't know about it."

You've turned to a page about inflation. A flyer for our high school's Gay-Straight Alliance is taped to one page.

"Remember this?" you murmur.

I do remember. The flyer is poorly designed and simple-looking, all black ink on white printer paper. During our senior year, the newly-formed Gay-Straight Alliance was trying to recruit members. You handed me this flyer and said we should go.

I said no. You never asked why, and I never told you.

"I remember," I reply.

"You said you didn't want to go."

"Yeah, that's because I didn't."

"Maybe you should have went."

You look concerned, but you shouldn't be. I don't know why you're bringing up this flyer from last year. It's been months since then. I've moved on.

"I know you felt terrible afterward," you continue. "I never brought it up, but I knew you were upset. I could tell you felt like you didn't belong anywhere."

The flyer stares up at me.

I hear the furnace kicking on.

"Eleanor," you say.

"I'm fine, Madeline. Stop it. I'm fine."

"Eleanor, please." You reach for my hand, but I move it away. "I'm sorry that I never said anything about this. But after the flyer, I realized that something was bothering you. You're afraid of yourself."

The house is silent. Steam rises from my bowl of soup. I can't think. All I can hear are my parents' whispers about Carter's *problems*. I remember those thoughts, those feelings like disease, that sickening dread that made me question what was wrong with me, why I didn't like boys, why I could never fit in. And I can remember Carter's texts. Central Park. My hand in yours. Questions you never asked. All the hints I never saw. There was a real meaning behind our escapades, my inviting you to Central Park, all our phone calls—I reached out to you because I was afraid of myself. I needed you to say that nothing was wrong with me. I believed that I could sneak out every weekend, never get caught, and nobody would know my secret.

I shake my head. The floorboards melt beneath my feet, warp, fall away. "No," I croak, and my voice cracks. "No, that can't be right."

Your eyes soften. You take my hands and I want to cry.

I thought Central Park was *your* escape, *your* refuge. Every time, I brought you there to get you away from your father. I never knew that it was me who needed a safe haven, me who needed a façade, me who needed the reassurance that I was completely normal.

"You were afraid of people knowing," you murmur. "Did you realize that, Eleanor?"

I don't know what I realized. I only know that I lived with myself for so long. I coexisted with lies. I breathed them. They told me that I could escape my feelings, act as if I was someone else and nobody would know.

"But nobody knew," I whisper. My words sound childish. I feel raw, cut open. My parents and everyone at school—I'm sure they knew. I'm sure they always knew. And I'm sure you knew you were providing me with an illusion. You knew that I found refuge in New York crowds, in the fact that nobody knew me. Every time you said not to worry, that our parents would never know—you knew that was what I wanted to hear.

"Eleanor," you say, "You know they did."

Our eyes meet and yours are brown, lighter than I remembered. "You need to get away from your father," I tell you. "Madeline, does he—does he still hurt you?"

You don't respond. I remember the first time you showed me your bruises. Blue and yellow, purple where they met. You hid them again and again, covered them up like a simple wound, pretended there was no blue beneath the bandage.

"Are you still hiding?" I ask, but you look away. "Do your college friends know?"

You draw in your lip.

We are silent for a long time.

"They don't know," you whisper.

Our hands are still together. I remember how we held hands last year. You were hurt; I was afraid of myself. But no matter how many months have passed, we haven't changed.

We are still pretending.

We are still an illusion.

"What about you?" you murmur. "Do your friends know about you?"

You know the truth: they don't. My mind is going back—to student groups waving rainbow flags, to my new friends who don't know the truth about me, to the girl in my chemistry class who I lend my notes, to the striped backpack pins that I try to ignore. I tell myself that I am normal, that I am not one of them. I shroud myself in a lie because I am terrified of what will happen if anyone sees who I truly am. And I tell myself that you can keep calling me, keep sending me text messages, keep telling me that I am normal, I am normal, I am normal.

My eyes tear up as you squeeze my hands. "I wasn't honest with you," you say. "Last year. I knew you were afraid. But I never asked if you were okay, and I never realized—I never realized that I was lying to myself too. When I collected the cars, I hoped I could escape from him. In school, I thought I could hide everything. In Central Park, I thought I was free."

We sit down at the table, our hands still together. The soup has gone cold. "I had a cousin," I rasp, and my voice sounds strange, as if I've never heard it before. "His name was Carter. He used to do everything with me. We played board games together." I squeeze my eyes shut. "He killed himself because he was gay. My uncle and aunt never knew that anything was wrong. Madeline, I wonder if he was covering up for everyone. I'm thinking—I'm thinking he lied to the world about himself. He hid and told himself that nobody would know."

I open my eyes.

"I don't want that to happen to you," I whisper.

You place your hand on my cheek. I'm talking about you, but I know I'm talking about myself too. While I'm terrified to have anyone find out about me, I know what scares me more: what will happen if I keep hiding.

"Eleanor," you tell me, "you have to face yourself."

I know we have to stop lying to each other. We have to stop lying to ourselves. I have to board a plane and go back to New York, face the person I am trying to hide. I have to find my own path.

You remove your hand from my cheek and place it in mine. "Tell me everything that hurts you," you say. "Tell me why you are so afraid of yourself."

There's no running from this now. I take a breath. I will tell you the truth about my secret. You will tell me the truth about diecast cars. For the first time, we will listen. We will look past the illusion and see ourselves.

Then we hear it: a car door slamming from outside.

"Who is that?" I ask.

"Mailman, probably," you answer.

A key jams into the front door and unlocks the first bolt, then the second. The greyhound barks. Your hands tighten around mine. We both know who it is.

It can't be him. He's supposed to be on a business trip. But you don't have any other relatives around here; nobody else has the house key but him.

We can't see the door from here. His boots thump against the floor and the greyhound's dog tags clink against each other and I know he sees my bag on the floor. My eyes meet yours and we clasp our hands together like we'll never let go.

"Madeline?" he calls.

In a few seconds, he will walk into the kitchen and find us.

Will we maintain the illusion? Will we succumb to him, to our veil, to our lie?

He steps into the room and your hands squeeze mine.

I hope we are strong enough.

Aging

Maddie Botti

We are three. We haven't been here for long, but we've already experienced more joy than our hearts know how to hold. We're running through a farm with bright, determined smiles on our faces. It's pouring, but we don't mind. Puddles burst beneath our feet as we sprint toward where our mothers stand, firm and definite. They are beacons of light, a sense of familiarity in this great big world we have yet to discover.

We are five. We sit at a rectangular table in a quaint tea shop, dressed in puffy floral dresses, hair spilling over our shoulders. An array of finger sandwiches lay in front of us along with delicate teacups, steam rising from the tops. We raise our pinkies as we lift them to our unblemished lips, and share secretive smiles over the brim. We are royal.

We are eight. We stand in the kitchen of a restaurant, passes dangling from our necks on lanyards. They make us feel special, as if we are part of some exclusive society. A chef reaches his tanned arms into the oven and removes the pizza we've created, placing it on the counter in front of us. I lean forward to get a closer look, resting my forearm horizontally on the edge of the counter. I barely have time to scream before my skin begins to bubble, heat tearing away at the outer layers. You try to make me laugh while I wait for my parents to arrive, arm soaking in a bucket of frigid water. I manage a smile through my tears. When I get home, I ask my dad if it will scar. He lies in his "no." This is the first of many.

We are eleven. It's one in the morning, and I hear your voice mingling with my mother's in the hall. She does not hate you yet. Sleep tempts me, but I force my mind awake, murmuring your name into the darkness. Lights blink on, and I see your face, pale and unsmiling. I ask what's wrong, and you tell me that your dad got sick. *How sick?* I wonder. You curl up next to me, shutting your eyes. It dawns on me that you might have to stay here for a while. I feel your tears on my pillow and a wrench in my heart.

We are thirteen. We are scintillating, brilliant, and bold. We are full of twisted thoughts of what the world is and what the world should be. We talk over each other loudly, standing in line for a roller coaster, the sun beating on our backs. I taste a curse word on my lips and throw it into our playful banter, a thrill rushing through me at the prospect of uttering something forbidden. You erupt into glorious laughter, and our hands brush. My face burns; it has nothing to do with the heat. Oh god, we are invincible.

We are fourteen. I jump off the bus and run into the coffee shop before the headlights of my mother's car can pick me out in the sea of faces. I race to the back, and there you are, long sleeves covering evidence of loneliness. The squeal you let out when you see me gives me hope for another chance: a version in which my parents don't find out and you stay happy. You hug me tightly; I feel it in my bones. I tell you I missed you, and you tell me you miss the days when my parents didn't hate you. Guilt washes over me, and I reach for your hand, but you pull out a picture of your boy. I allow jealousy to sting me for a moment, and then I am clinging to you as if you are the only thing keeping me here, murmuring a quick goodbye into your shoulder. The cold air cuts me open when I step outside.

We are fifteen. I haven't seen you in a year. So much has happened since then, and some of it is your fault, but most of it is not. I think of you often, though we don't talk much anymore. Our conversations are full of words that have lost their meaning, like "I miss you" and "if only." Sometimes I see the jagged white lines on your wrists when I picture you, and dread fills me to the point of panic. This is when my dad comes into my room and tells me everything is going to be okay while rubbing my back as if I am a lamp, and if he wishes hard enough, I will be normal. But other times, I see your eyes, the color of seafoam and emeralds. I wonder, briefly, what you see when you think of me.

We are sixteen. I've been sitting in this straight-backed chair for five hours, listening to the beeping of your heart, watching you fade in and out. My parents think I'm asleep at my grandmother's house, but I am worlds away from there. The girl before me is not the one I once knew, but then, we are both a far cry from who we used to be. I've been reading to you softly for what could be forever, my voice steadily growing hoarse, but I don't stop. Your eyes are closed, and I realize that if this is the end, I will never see them again. Selfishly, I call your name. I watch them snap open. I stare for a long time.

We are seventeen. You've done it again, and now you're on the ground, bleeding. You beg me not to call for help, but my hands shake as I dial my last hope for your life. You tell me you love me, and I plead, "Don't leave me." Your eyelids flutter recklessly, dangling hope before my eyes.

My shoulders shake as I vomit violent sobs. You shush me until I'm quiet. You're gasping for air now. I can see that your body wants to hold on, but your mind gave up somewhere between girl and woman. Tears tumble down my cheeks; you beckon me closer. I lower my ear to your lips. You whisper, "I'm going back to the farm."

MAGIC HANDS

NICOLE LI

back then, there existed
    the strangest things.
        (like a
      shoelace-tying
    contest where the
  winner really
got nothing at
all except
bragging
  rights)
    I don't know
      what made me try so hard—
        perhaps the warm, wrinkled
              hands
              on mine
           as they looped
        in and out,
      over and under,
    smooth and well-oiled
  as the subway
tracks
    under our apartment.
      soon, there would be a
        perfect bow where
          previously existed
            only a heap of
        dirty fiber.
      when I did
    it myself,
      the ropes became
        unwieldy snakes,
          slippery and

sly as soap
in too-
wet hands.

I decided this
was the only magic
I needed, the
type of Cinderella
transformation
you
hear about
on TV.

And my
grandfather:
a fairy Godmother
with magic hands
instead of wand.

STATIC

MATHILDA BARR

she waits.
afternoon forgets to breathe
cul de sac decay, sun stinks up the sky
the putrid silence shoved down her throat meant to go down like

water only it's
orange cream popsicle tears dripping puddles on the porch
the world is asphalt and stucco
she can't remember what they told her to say it's all static
static
driving down the freeway the radio louder and louder its thunder
in her ears she can't look she can't speak all that exists is her and
light and speed and sound and everything is alive and then
static

if she drives fast enough maybe it will all melt
eighty degrees plastered smiles melt with the summer heat
static
eighty-five sticky august dreams slide down to the pavement
static
ninety family dinner smashed china on the living room floor
gasoline tears
static
ninety-five bitter lies melt until truth is just exposed flesh she
lights a match
static
one hundred
everything that exists is her and light and speed and sound and
everything is alive and she can't feel anything except the knowing,
the craving the hating august is burning

their perfect concrete jungle
suburbia is ablaze

Romeo craves
fifteen minutes of fame

Cathleen Weng

I crush irony between my palms to make Technicolor
powder that you force down your throat and
swallow dry. It glows between your teeth in the night like
a blood-stained wolf smile. You call me a god, the
purest thing you have ever corrupted and you
beg me to spend one more hazy cicada midnight
in your dingy motel room with the low-hanging
Shakespearean light. Verona cuts your
tongue with whiskey, jars it between bitten
termite holes in the cupboard, an acrid exchange
for infamy. I leave before morning arrives.

Loss Tastes Like McDonald's

Patrick Wang

Loss lives life to the fullest, and he never stops—long walks on
the beach, bottles of Hennessy, frisky women—he's seen it all.
Loss will take you out at his club Insomnia, feed you
tequila shots with lime wedges and make you dance till you
forget that you're 50% alcohol and 50% regret. Sometimes
you might run into him at the spa, steaming his face with
the vapors of makeshift communities. He'll ask you to
join, and when you do, your eyes will fog up with dreams in
languages made obsolete through forgetfulness or violence
or sometimes both. After one or two drinks, he'll lean in for
the kiss. Funny—he still probably tastes like Big Macs and
hash browns from that new McDonald's in your parents'
hometown two oceans away.

Loss speaks in forgotten tongues, wears cologne that cleaves the air
like a fading memory. Sometimes, he pulls the training wheels off
children's bicycles—watches them fall—because why not? *It's fun.* But
don't you go thinking that Loss isn't fair. He says that he
doesn't discriminate against anyone. Young children, young
adults, old adults—no one escapes his company.

Loss is a master of seduction, likes to beckon at you with his finger.
Coax you into playing his game of show and tell. Show him a tragedy
and he'll tell you that it never gets better. Then he'll add your
tragedy to his bag. Another piece for his collection. At night,
Loss inspects the day's haul—keys, v-cards, marbles (physical),
marbles (metaphorical), loved ones, memories of said loved ones, abandoned
Happy Meal toys—and puts them into neatly labeled boxes inscribed with
owners' names. And yet, after a long day of work, whilst lying in
bed, Loss looks up at the ceiling and feels empty because, truth is,
Loss is a lonely guy. He's had affairs with thousands of
people, but everyone always gets tired of his games; eventually

Time puts out the fires he starts.

Loss is tired of his monotonous job but
doesn't know how to retire. If you look closely, in the corner
of his house, there is a small wooden box inscribed with his name.
He's still too afraid to open it.

JUICEBOX LOVE AFFAIR

Sarah Uhlman

silica gel: "do not eat," throw away,
not suitable for consumption.
kids like us would down our capri suns to cover the taste
of sour-tasting, chalky pills too big to swallow, and
our tiny lungs would soak up the toxicity of the second-hand
addiction that permeated the bodies around us.
we hate authority only because we're still small enough
to fit so snugly in their palms,
but also because no one can tell us what to do.
we call bullshit in whispers, because if we shouted it
like every band-aid covered bone in our body meant it,
we would get punished for cussing.
we hide our parents' money in our clenched fists
so our friends think we can afford to smoke too,
we melt in the summer like the cds
we always played in the car on road trips.
our thighs don't burn any more from the
hot metal slides at the elementary school a block
away, they burn because of what happened after the
last scars of childhood faded and
our smooth skin was made rough
by years of a childhood that never happened
like it should have.

WHEN THE ROSE BLOOMED

ANNA CARSON

How long had it been since the rose had bloomed?

Surely the last time was millennia ago, when rain fell from the
sky like falling diamonds,
as clear and hard and certain as ignorance.
Many years, countless, when the grass was as green as naïveté
and the garden still harbored hope for a sunny morning.
But now the stone held like stubborn, a grey and demanding
wall that never rested.
A tower that screamed at its inhabitants bustling
in, out, in and out, up and down

to hurry or stop and keep moving for as long as possible.

How long had it been since the rose had bloomed?
At least a week, a worrisome week.
The petals as lifeless as knowledge,
the stem a gritty green.
Seven days of lost luck and blissful torture,
for the soil was undoubtedly screaming in the rotting water that
chained its twisted roots.

How long had it been since the rose had bloomed?

Centuries of desert dry,
a land that hadn't seen life
until a bud of blood dripped hot and wet upon the bones of
regret.
When earth still held innocence like a
child holds rain on the tip of the tongue,
the way snow rests light and icy on the fir tree's branch.
When the flower didn't cry tears of lost joy,

when the wind was as clean and crisp as the child's laugh,
when life was long and unfettered.
When refusal to see the obvious was but a dream,

That was when the flower bloomed.

When the marigold opened its eyes and the lily unfurled,
when the poppy reached toward morning dew and
a bright future and
a chance at living a happy life.

When did the rose bloom?

It bloomed at love and birth and new beginnings.
As sun rays laughed at daydream imaginings,
verdant bones straighten and
color blossoms like excitement for the new day.

That is when the rose bloomed.

It bloomed years ago,
in the time of lost aspirations and dreary nightmares,
it was the crimson sight on which we latched in desperate need
of comfort.

But we have not seen the rose bloom for a very long time.
And I doubt we ever will.

THE SHOPLIFTER

DEDEEPYA GUTHIKONDA

Asab reached for the lighters, intentionally fiddling with the basket, making his movements known, but not too obvious. He pretended to be a regular customer, grabbing a few lighters and pausing, attempting to assess them with trivial standards. He let the pile of lighters slip from his hand until there were only two remaining, and made a swift movement, his left hand sliding them into the back pocket of his baggy jeans. The lighters were jumbo-sized and fit just right, settling into the crease on the bottom half of his pocket. The familiar smell of smoke clung to him, wafting into his nose as he pulled his hood tighter around his face, and glanced behind at the register.

The man behind the counter was conversing eagerly with a woman who didn't seem to be interested. She provided only the occasional, subtle nod, one that was forced simply out of fear of awkwardness. A thick accent coated the owner's voice, making his English sound choppy, yet deliberate. It reminded Asab of his own, during the rare times when he spoke. In retrospect, he realized that was what had drawn him to the store. He reasoned he could take advantage of the owner's seemingly vulnerable state, believing he would be drawn to trusting a familiar face like his own, someone from the same country. Specks of guilt blotted that idea, but he attempted to gloss it over with the fact that he considered himself to be torn apart, broken, and quite frankly a bad person. He lifted his eyes from the owner and glanced at what the lady was buying—keychains and candy bars, postcards and various tubes of lotion and perfume. Next to this cluttered pile of objects were not one, but two cases of beer. Last-minute Christmas gifts, and plenty to celebrate for afterwards, he assumed. He had never ceased to notice the little things—a skill that was required for his craft.

Judging from the looks of it, he had time to snag one more thing. The store owner went through the price tag on each item,

55

sticking to an old-fashioned way of writing the numbers down and adding them up, occasionally stopping to push his glasses up over the bridge of his nose. Perfect.

Asab adjusted his hood to cover the side of his face and used the sole of his shoes to spin around, a habit he had grown up with. The metal chain on his neck slightly rattled, syncopating with his spin. He eyed the mini-fridge full of beer cans and water bottles. Those were too risky. He instead turned into the next aisle and his eyes scoured for something he could eat for dinner, although it was almost midnight. He searched for the kind of ramen he used to get at his last store before the store owner had threatened to call the police and kicked him out. The funny thing was, Asab had paid for everything at that store. The owner had been a man whose skin resembled the pale, uncooked noodles he had been purchasing at the time. But that was a long time ago, too long to think about. It was a time before he was living on the streets of New York City.

He pushed away this unwanted memory and the ramen that came with it and picked up a pack of chips instead, salt and vinegar—the only thing that would end up on the checkout counter. As the woman left the store, she sent the bells hung up on the door instantly chattering away into the night, provoking a startled Asab who instantly jerked away from the chips. It was out of habit, the fear that lurked in his craft that he hadn't overcome yet. He looked up. The store owner was rustling with some papers, bending down to pick up a scattered pile that had danced their way to the ground from the gush of cold, bitter air that had come racing in. He was an aged man—in his sixties probably. He brought back vague memories of Asab's own father back home. This thought left him astounded, as easily as it loitered in the back of his head. He had tried to forget about his father ever since he left Syria. Forgetting was the easiest thing he could do. It was the only thing he knew how to do. So he tried to stop thinking about Syria, his home. Until friends and family had become a salty afterthought from the past.

"Hello!" the owner cheerily called to Asab. "Can I help you?"

Shoot. He made the slightest movement with his head, invisible under the hoodie. He could feel the owner's eyes on him for a couple more seconds, burning into his scalp, tension building up in his veins. "Let me know if I can help you!" he said once again, his tone and energy unchanged by Asab's lacking response.

He couldn't go check out right now, they had made an unexpected interaction. Asab dragged his feet across the floor as if he was burdened with heavy weights attached. He took a look outside, peering up from a shelf full of postcards. Flashing Christmas lights were the only thing saving the streets from utter, dark despair. A sort of eerie silence lurked in the air, interrupted only by the occasional footsteps or rattle on the sidewalks. The world yelled *Christmas*, everywhere except this store. This store whispered *Syria*, to him. The whole atmosphere of it. It was the closest he had ever felt to home. Without even realizing it, he felt a change in his heart—something that felt like it could be warm. It shocked him, making his heart pound faster as he tried to figure out what this strange feeling was. That was when he heard their voices.

It happened incredibly quickly.

One moment, yells and shouts were heard in the otherwise empty, silent streets. The rattling, squeaky turning of bike wheels blasted through the air. The next, a slur, a phrase, that he had heard much too often. And then, something shattered, it had come flying through the air and Asab had ducked, the same rush of adrenaline he got when he feared he would be caught rushed through his bones faster than ever. The voices turned into laughter—cruel, drunken laughter that echoed through the streets. *Go back to your country. Get your ass out of ours.*

Asab stayed ducked for a long time. His arms covered his head and he held them there, tightly. His heart was sprinting away and pounded everywhere it wasn't supposed to. His fingers burned and tingled until he could no longer feel them, just as he could no longer feel any sense of control or sanity or even the state of being. His eyes were squeezed shut, harder than they were supposed to be, pressing down and warping his eyelids into the shape of almonds. His breath came out shakily, in halted beats, sending him gasping inwardly for a single bite of air. His mind was disconnected from his body, flooding him with the feeling he was up in the air floating. He knew something bad was going to happen. He envisioned buildings falling, cement landing and crackling down, sirens blasting and screams, from men and children alike. He heard sounds of bombs and the screeching of fire, the deceiving smell of smoke invading his every sense, choking him until he fell down, clasping his stomach and begging for mercy. His hands went down to his feet and he gritted his knuckles, punching the ground. His eyes remained closed. Suddenly, he felt a hand on his shoulder, softly, gently pulling itself up.

"Hey," it said softly, the same cheerfulness as before appeared more subtle, but lurking in the voice, nonetheless.

Asab opened his eyes. He found himself staring at the mini-fridge again, full of water bottles and beer cans. He felt the hand slide slowly off his shoulder and could see the store owner next to him. His pack of salt and vinegar chips was lying to his side. He mumbled something, in shock and embarrassment.

"It happens," the owner said. "It's happened to me too." He said this quietly, still gazing right at him.

Asab looked at him. "I've tried so hard to forget," he said, his lip trembling and his voice shaky. He hadn't talked in so long. The owner chuckled.

"If you try so hard to forget, you will only remember," he said, his eyes sparkling. Asab could see crease marks on his face, marks that his endless smiles had probably left behind.

"Forgetting is hard for those who have heart," the owner said, delicately, opening the mini-fridge and pulling out a bottle of water. He screwed the top open and handed it to Asab, who hesitated for a second, startled. No one had ever handed him anything like that, so easily, before.

"Take it," the owner persuaded. Asab took the water and gulped it down in one sip. The cold tinge brought him back to his senses.

"Thank you," Asab said, crushing the plastic in his hand. He stood up. The owner walked him away from the aisles, where the damage was visible. A window had shattered. Shards and specks of glass dotted the floors, sprinkled all over. They were costumed as something beautiful, but evil lurked behind their fluorescent gaze. Two rocks, the size of baseballs, jagged and sharp, lay slightly farther away from the glass. These were what had come flying in, carrying hate in all forms, crushing and destroying everything in its path. As Asab looked at the trail of glass, he realized something.

The owner had been directly across from the window. The two rocks had come flying at him. One wrong move, and . . . he took another shaky breath. He didn't want to think about it.

"Sorry about that," Asab muttered. The owner took a deep breath in. "Oh," he said, pausing faintly. Asab saw a change in his eyes, a look that flooded his face for less than a second. He went back to flicking his hand as if it was no big deal. "It's nothing. I'm grateful for my life!" he said lightheartedly, still joking. Asab smiled, and then stopped when he felt the turn of his lips against his rigid skin.

"I should get going," he said.

"Hold on."

Asab watched him step over the glass and scribble something on a piece of paper. The owner looked straight at him as he handed him the odd slip.

"Call me," he said. "I was in your place not too many years ago."

"Oh."

"I need some help in the store," he said. Asab nodded. He didn't know what to think. He shifted uneasily on his heels a few times, and eventually headed towards the front door. The lighters were still in his pocket. He paused, the shards of glass reflecting in his eyes.

"Wait," he mumbled and reached for his back pocket.

"Ah," the store-keeper laughed once again. They locked eyes for a quick second until Asab broke their gaze.

"Keep them." The storekeeper said, flicking his hand out into the air again. Asab opened his mouth, shocked, but he closed it before anything had a chance to slide off his tongue. The look on the storekeeper's face, and the flicker of *something* in his eye, and he knew. The storekeeper knew.

Asab stood there in shock and embarrassment, shifting on his feet, unsteadily. The storekeeper handed him the pack of salt and vinegar chips.

"Take these with you too."

Asab took them and stood there a little awkwardly. His face was a dark shade of red under his black hood and he wasn't sure how to refuse. He mustered up a subtle nod to the store owner and pushed open the door, sending the bells once again prattling into the cold night air. Only this time, Asab didn't mind it.

He breathed in the cool night air and glanced at the piece of paper. He folded it carefully and put it into his back pocket with the lighters.

The corner of his mouth turned up slightly and this time, he let it stay there. White specks came floating down and brushed his shoulders and cheeks.

It was Christmas indeed.

THEY LET ME PASS

MAIA SIEGEL

On the sidewalk up ahead
Under the belly of the bridge
Is a man with a painted-white face.
His hands, too, are covered in white paint.
*Did he want to see if he could white
himself out of existence?* He is crouching, rocking
Back and forth, praying. I have seen enough
Horror movies to know that this is end-times.
I get out my phone to pretend to call someone,
But I end up just silently pressing the dark glass
To my ear, as if it could somehow mute this man
Vibrating under the belly of the bridge. He does not
Register my presence, and these are not end-times.
Four men emerge from the dark with beers
And it is end-times again. Until they, too, let me pass.
I emerge with a red ear and a palpitation. They let me pass.
A mantra: *They Let Me Pass. they let me pass. They did.*
The belly of the bridge swallows them whole,
Like they are Jonah in the whale.

HERE IS THE CHURCH
AND HERE IS THE STEEPLE

Sarah Uhlman

my jesus died for sunday morning bacon,
the mixed fabric in the dress i wore to church last week,
my sister, her girlfriend, and almost everyone else i know.
my jesus had dark skin, darker hair, and even darker eyes—
i think he looked a little bit like jason momoa
and that image always comforted me.
i had always viewed Him through a microscope of sorts,
reading between the lines and analyzing like
i'd find salvation in between the double spaces—
after all, they told me that i would—
but my understanding of your words was only fragmentary
and i started to make Him in my image.
i was named, "noblewoman," "princess,"
the counterparts of which being,
"nobleman, prince."
but i am no sarah, i am no abraham.
i am, in fact, more of an eve;
a raw rib cage barely held together by tendons and fig leaves,
sore from laughing, sore from the womanly duties
i felt i *had* to perform for you, my dearest adam.
my first man.
i've been molded into this since the day i was
dropped from no one's womb, covered in beautiful,
bruised, pink skin and decorated with full lips,
scars, stretches, a thousand slopes
too steep for any one person to climb on their own.
i've often found myself wondering why the nomenclature
of the man, the woman, and the snake is so different
when they all must crawl on their bellies to reach
whichever hellish shape they dragged
their heavy bodies from
when they tasted that fruit for the first time.

we tasted it first as we tasted each other,
so sweet and wet and faulted but it felt *human*—
an innocent humanity in which you would worship me,
break bread over my broken body
and yours would dance on its own
when i touched your rough skin.
so ugly on our own, but—so beautiful together.
we would make water into wine with our tongues,
being drunk on those already hazy nights;
and when i wanted everything else,
you would give your ambrosia
without hesitation.
i worshiped you too, then, a sadist god
who would cater to my masochism,
craving suffering and i hoping that you would suffer too.
i believe you are polylingual in my many love languages,
you speak in tongues with your
tongue's movements in the dark,
pushing through the thin skin between us,
protecting us;
crushing our pits into one another.
you tell me that you like how we can speak
without saying anything at all.
i think to myself,
you just don't want me to say out loud anything
you'd be afraid of hearing.

WHITE LADY ETUDE

KEVIN KONG

From the Chinese legend of the White Snake

Bridge. Of immortal selling pills,
sesame-stuffed tangyuan. Of poor who

desire jade & remain hidden to spirits.
We are wrapped of serpents &

forever bonded as caduceus.
Our fates swept away. Under the

raindrops of my country: heartache spirits.
Chemicals surge in him & are

unyellow. Because, she says,
I am reflected of a mirror &

horrid. Tremors come
before shocks, shed skin-tight.

Ravel out this opportunity.
She knows waves crash in

my chest. Chamber protecting a
heart that beats of children's cries.

Fate's softshell, permeable to a
vicious bite. Anti-venom threatened.

Cowering, an orange tint,
weakness-stained.

RABBIT LUCK

NICOLE LI

Sometimes it's hard to picture mom—a porcelain girl, lost and determined somewhere in the middle of China.

Today, our sticky Ikea table has been revamped, cheap surface haphazardly hidden under a gingham tablecloth. Mother plucks the cap off a pot of jasmine tea. Refills her cup, laughing at all the appropriate times at a colleague's story of a disastrous Himalayan hiking trip. A fly buzzes drunkenly around the fruit platter, escaping my half-hearted bats. Next to me, Gerald's boredom roils off of him in waves.

"*Professor Chan*" he mouths at me, and I grin. He's right—right now this woman is not our mother, but rather Sylvia Chan, Tenured Professor at The University Of Central Florida. The signs are all there. Rouged mouth stretched uncomfortably wide. Hands pertly folded. Crisp blouse buttoned to the throat.

I'd never liked it when mom's colleagues came over for brunch, and Gerald even less. Said it made him sick to eat so much smoked salmon in one go, but I knew it was something else.

"Isa, can we go outside?" a pleading tug at my shirt cuff. I pretend not to hear him, though we both know I'll cave soon. So we go.

Outside, the sun swelters and settles like cotton candy in our lungs the way only Florida heat knows how. I'm about to scold my brother for dragging us out into the sickly humidity when I see *nai nai* bent over her strawberry patch, stiff hip forgotten for the moment. Upon seeing us, she beckons with a single gloved hand.

"Look what those damn rabbits do this time," She twirls the stem of a single strawberry between thumb and forefinger accusingly, sunlight illuminating its mutilated sides, "never have this problem in Sichuan."

"Don't worry, I'll make them pay." Gerald declares this solemnly, like he'll really hunt the creature down in its burrow and threaten it until it coughs up a syrupy pulp.

I think our grandma must secretly like stuffing them fat and full, because once she told us a story about the lucky rabbit that lives in the moon and how it got there because it sacrificed its own body to an old hungry beggar. The gods were so moved that they sent it to the moon and made it immortal.

I've never quite been able to swallow these tall tales the way she does, wholly and reverently.

We spend the rest of the morning carefully trimming around the edges of the fruits until they're almost perfect little crescents. Finally, *nai nai* declares them good as new, pops one of them in her mouth. Gerald eagerly follows suit, and soon they're downing the moon-berries one after another until there's only one left.

"Isa?" they both look at me, and I pause, can only think about the dirt under our nails and the rabbits' sour breath. My brother squints like he knows what I'm thinking, but only reaches out and plucks the last strawberry.

***

The sky is dark when I see *nai nai* fall onto her knees in the garden a few weeks later, stiff and upright like a sinner praying for salvation. The night air is moist, the trill of nearby cicadas deafening. They hide her grimace and cry of surprise well.

"What's going on, *nai nai*?"

"Ah, flowers smell better from here. Don't you know?" I don't, but I believe her. Because *nai nai* never lies. Because *nai nai* is sure-footed as a lynx and never falls, so this must be the only explanation.

"Come see yourself if you don't trust me, *qin ai de.*" My dear.

I hesitate, think of rotten, dying, crawling things in the grass. In my head, Gerald calls me a pussy. So I walk over and lower myself onto my knees until we're mirroring each other.

But of course she's right—here, the heady fragrance of the nearby rose bushes threatens to overwhelm me. It mingles with a hundred other scents. Peonies, daffodils, hydrangeas, and other plants I don't know the name of. Mom tried hard to make this place a home. I breathe in deep, strangely relieved.

Suddenly, nai nai stretches her arms out and falls on her back with a whoop. Her white hair all puffed out on the dirt and her arms sweeping over the earth, winglike, turn her into a bird trying to take flight. And it's somehow the funniest thing I've ever seen so I start laughing and can't stop and I fall backwards too.

Gerald finds us like that, making snow angels in the dirt until I can't remember why I'm down here. When he reaches down to pull *nai nai* up, she grips him like a baby. Hard enough that I see finger-shaped imprints on his skinny forearms afterwards.

***

My brother gets his nose in a lot of places it shouldn't be. He was the one who discovered that the family trip to Orlando a few years ago wasn't just so we could meet Mickey Mouse. That was back when we lived in a Chinatown in New Jersey and mom was a poor grad student waiting tables on the side like all the other poor grad students.

I had been lathering on my fourth layer of sunscreen when mom finally emerged from the hotel bathroom in a crisp white blouse, black blazer, and one of those pencil skirts they wear on lawyer shows. She stretched her rouged lips wide, and Professor Chan made her first appearance. Gerald squinted.

"What's so important that you'd skip *Disney*?" He said Disney like it was something holy, and it kind of was. The closest thing we'd experienced was going to the county fair the year before with our fat cousin from China who had eaten deep fried Oreos until she puked. Mom only smiled and said nothing.

My hands were still covered in cotton candy when we returned to the hotel room in the evening. Mom was there, still in her formalwear. She clasped her hands together like a schoolgirl and gushed, *gushed* about how she was going to be an assistant professor at the local University, how the interview went so well, how we could go to Disney every weekend once we moved here, all in a continuous breath.

But I wasn't thinking anything except how hard melted sugar was to get off your fingers because how was I supposed to know that on that day, Mother was split in two. That the new one would learn a sitcom laugh and invite old white people over for brunch and read *Architectural Digest* to build us a white picket fence house in a picket white fence town.

The layers of sunscreen hadn't worked. My skin peeled off in strips for weeks, just another thing that was no longer Chinese about me.

***

The flowers are supposed to be shedding their petals already. It's the beginning of October, yet they remain pert and cheerful. Somehow it infuriates me, how even nature defies nature here. Mom's working late again, and Gerald and *nai nai* are nowhere to be seen. I feel like I should have somewhere to be too, but I don't.

Nai nai comes home holding a plastic shopping bag with a yellow smiley face and *Have a Nice Day!* printed on it. I recognize it from the Asian supermarket. She pulls out something hard and vacuum-sealed. Mooncakes—it must be Mid-Autumn festival today. Offers me one tentatively, and I accept.

Zhōng qiū jié kuài lè, we chant, knocking the pastries together. *Happy Mid-Autumn festival.* This sounds like a lie too, like we're playing a part. The mooncakes taste exactly how I remember, dusty and flavorless. But what can you expect from the frozen section of some dingy store in America.

***

Nai nai searches for summer in December. At breakfast, she suddenly stands up and slides open the screen door. I watch her shuffle past the rose bushes and peonies and daffodils, stopping beside her strawberry patch. Right now, the plants are bare and stiff, buds tucked into themselves for the winter. She stretches her hands towards the ground and my hands tense as if ready to catch a falling thing. Then she's searching the tops and bottoms of the plants, each leaf and each stem. As the seconds pass her search grows more frantic.

She returns wild, mutters something like *where are my strawberries, must be the rabbits again, little thieves all of them,* and I don't know what scares me more, the manic light in her eyes or the fact that she thinks strawberries should be growing six months past their season. I say *it's okay it's winter and the rabbits are in their burrows just like the strawberries but they'll come back next spring and it will all be okay,* but it's just as much for me than her.

***

"How long has she been gone?" Mom asks, even though she must know because she always asks questions she knows the answer to like that will change the truth.

"Three hours, maybe," Gerald offers.

"She tell you where she was going?"

"Nah, not really. Maybe the Asian supermarket? Sure she's okay though."

Nai nai likes taking afternoon walks like all old people, though what she sees in this rundown shoulder of a neighborhood I'll never know. Three hours is past the acceptable length of time for any kind of walk, but no one moves. If I close my eyes for a moment, I see her bending over a storm sewer on the way home, admiring a dandelion that has pushed its way through the concrete slats. Blooming against all odds. She will think of her own daughter and how she reminds her of the dandelion. *Nai nai* is taking the long way home, groceries in the crook of an elbow. Whistling one of those old Chinese tunes she used to sing to me before she said her voice was too old and scratchy for an audience. I see this so clearly that it becomes the truth.

What really happens is this: *nai nai* can't find her way home. We find her two streets away waiting on a stone bench like she's exactly where she means to be, like we're the ones late to a meeting.

"Mother, there you are," mom says with her Professor voice, "enjoying the weather, I see."

Grandma nods like *yes, the sun is beautiful today,* like she hadn't just forgotten a route worn old and tired by her own feet.

But I've been learning how to catch things like the trembling in her legs as she slides off the bench, so I'm not fooled again.

***

She's a good liar. I wonder if she always has been. I wonder if her feet have always dangled above the sidewalk like this, if her eyes have always hung milky with cataracts. If, after all this, I'm the blind one.

***

The little things hit me. How clean it smells—the air is thick with it, this strange pine-tree-Clorox-first-winter scent. The squeaking of the floor as I step foot into the lobby. The pearly smile 'Hi My Name is Amber' flashes at us from behind a tall receptionist's counter.

"Hello, we're here for Deborah Chan."

We follow Amber down a few long corridors, colorful posters flitting at us from both sides. *Discover Your Inner Yogi*, one declares, while another trumpets that *Friday Bingo is the New Black*. Finally, Amber stops in front of one of the dozens of doors lining the hallway. Opens it, and there she is. There's a single thin metal bed in the center of the room, and my grandma is tucked into it like one of the china dolls she gave me when I was younger. The reception lady walks right up next to the bed, pats the top of her head. *Deborah has been doing just great, haven't we*, Amber says, but I can barely hear her. Mother insisted on a new name for *nai nai* when she determined Rui An was too much of a mouthful for certain tongues to twist around. But hearing it coming out of this woman's mouth just makes me think of PTSA moms and crocheting, when nai nai deserves secret gardens and rabbits in the moon.

"Well, I'll be in the lobby," Amber says.

Nai nai looks the same. Her hands cupping each other like doves over the sheets. Hair just as white and wild as when we last saw her. But I suddenly can't think of anything to say.

"Don't you look cozy," Mom says, "how are you?"

"Good. Good food here but not enough Chinese."

"Yeah I know you can't go long without your jiaozi. You should teach Isa how to make them next time! Wow, you got a nice view."

"Best in whole building." *Nai nai's* smile is proud.

They're both avoiding the elephant squeezing all the air out of the room. If I have to listen to a second more of this I might explode just like a water balloon. *Nai nai* shows us around—the swimming pool, the garden, the cafeteria. All of it smells the same. Old people and Axe. And through it all, a terrible *offness* pervades the air, slipping in our noses and behind our collarbones.

The car ride back is silent but for mother's animated babbling about the weather and how she would also like a vacation like *nai nai*, the lucky bastard.

"Just say she has dementia," Gerald says venomously, "I mean everyone goes batshit crazy at some point. Part of life, right?" Mother recoils like a slingshot, and I am sickly satisfied.

***

The strawberries are the worst part. Rabbits in the juice, rabbits in the moon. Summer is a reminder of what we lost. In the Chinese tales, the gods always reveal themselves to the deserving in their darkest of times. So where is her immortality, her jade prince, her palace in the clouds? Maybe Florida stomped it out like it stomped everything else out. Instead, we will watch her skin curdle and mind bend into itself until she forgets her own name and all the stupid stories that couldn't save her.

When mother's colleagues come over for brunch again, neither Gerald nor I bring up going outside. I am a porcelain girl to mother's perfect porcelain woman. Even if we tried, I don't think either of us could manage anything more. Besides, there is nothing worth going out into the sickly heat for. Let the little beasts glut themselves on fruit until they swell and burst. Let the roses grow a wall around the garden so thorny that they poison themselves.

BALLOONS DON'T BELONG
IN HEAVEN

Julia Do

mama thought she didn't belong here on earth
because nothing here made her smile
so she tried to fly up to the heavens
like an angel maybe
no not an angel
more like a helium balloon because
balloons don't belong in heaven
they belong here
on earth
and i was so little when mama tried to fly away
that i had to tiptoe
to reach the end of her string
to yank her back down to earth so hard that
she could never fly away again

but my mama's like helium
and helium sneaks away
bit by bit
day by day
'til she's all gone.

THE DAY MY MOTHER SOLD MY PIANO

CYNTHIA WANG

The day my mother sold my piano,
I felt her uproot my veins and hold my
fingers hostage. And suddenly,
the clouds that looked like personified dreams
just yesterday became fish spines and
rib cages—hollow music staffs. The clear sky
that looked like soft, blue silk became empty
sheet music—lonely pages with no
song to sing.

I stood in the shadow of my piano, wrists
unshackled, but fingers torn from the
stem like plucked daisies. I've heard
of musicians who wished to hook their
fingers into the atriums of their hearts:
to pump music from their organs, just as
how one breathes through an accordion.

I unraveled my arteries and strew
them along worn, stained songs. My
tissues became time signatures and
my capillaries morphed into cadenzas.
I found melodies in my skin and
harmonies in my muscles. Learnt the whispers
of my lungs. Dissected my body into a hall
of honor.

Your eyelashes are the fibers of violin strings.
Your taste buds are the brass keys
of a saxophone. Your body is just as
wondrous as Beethoven's symphonies. You
are Music: worthy of worship.

BUTTERFLIES

PIA BHATIA

on the street in Chennai
next to the sleeping tail of a street dog
I see half a butterfly—
it lies in the earth, damp with waste and jagged with apathy
its other wing carried away by road

the next morning, I find one under my pillow
for a moment I hope it is just sleeping, softness pressed together
like a newborn's eyelids
this is not the case,
dead again.
I just want to go home

seagulls for fallen soldiers
owls for old women who died in their beds
doves for girls who never found love but at least found peace
I dream of willows weeping cold morning rain that lives for days

sleet on every *mogra*
that ruin this dirty city with their loveliness
more half-dead half-butterflies
this season's graveyard, and all I did was watch.

I WISH

TIFFANY LIU

I wish I weren't Asian. I wish that my ethnicity didn't evoke images of identical looking, small eyed, flat faced, yellow skinned mathematicians who can't drive. They say the key to happiness is to be yourself, but how can that be true if my identity is to blame for leaving me with nothing but insecurity and self-doubt?

"Chink," my classmate haughtily mocks, a faint smile playing on his lips. Unfazed, I offer a light-hearted giggle and a gentle push on his shoulder.

"Ching-Chong," I chant along with my American friends, laughing at their attempts to mimic the accent of an Asian foreigner.

"I can't see, I'm Asian," I joke, successfully eliciting a few chuckles from my peers as I dramatically squint to read the words on the whiteboard.

While my seeming liveliness and light-hearted self-mockery likely radiates confidence and self-assurance, it's all a disguise: a mere mask to conceal the vulnerable girl who hides underneath, desperately holding to what's left of her morale.

Never would I have thought on that bleak January morning when my English teacher, accompanied with the usual chorus of groans and complaints, distributed copies of the new assigned reading, that it would so profoundly alter my entire perspective. Yet Inside Out and Back Again, a verse novel written as the diary of Ha, a ten-year-old Vietnamese girl who escapes to find refuge in America, became for me a torch in the darkness of self-doubt.

... [my teacher] shows photographs
... of Vietnam,
   of green mountains and long beaches, of a statue of the Buddha reclining. She asks me,
      'Would you like to say anything?'

   'I know Buddha'

I hear laughter
and a murmur building:
Boo-Da, Boo-da" (Lai 205).

My eyes absorbed the black print and my mind lurched back to my third grade art class. Worse than any stumble on the concrete playground or any prick of the finger on my mother's sewing needle, scorching humiliation inflamed my entire body as my American classmates mocked me: "Boo-Dist, What a weird name!" Their childish laughter set fire to my cheeks while their smiles were daggers in my young and fragile self-esteem. Between absentmindedly painting geometric shapes on white construction paper, religion had arisen as the topic of conversation and I had excitedly rushed to tell them my family practiced Buddhism. As one of four Asians in my elementary school, I suddenly felt myself shriveling among my classmates who so very conspicuously had no idea what being a "Buddhist" signified.

Just a few days later, still raw from art class, I encountered that same burn of embarrassment. The sensation struck upon watching the cartoon, *The Magic School Bus,* and I sunk into my seat as the heat creeped its way from the center of my face to the tips of my ears. In the dark classroom the only light came from the television, illuminating the faces of my classmates with an eerie blue; my face must have emitted another color just as bright. Previously, I had loved the treat of watching The Magic School Bus, but this time was different. Sitting there in that classroom felt more like a punishment. I was embarrassed. Embarrassed whenever Wanda, the Asian cartoon character, appeared on screen. Embarrassed by her flat nose, upturned eyes, and nasally voice. Was that what people thought of me? My newfound insecurity had taken the best of me and in that moment, it felt as if everyone was staring. I wished nothing more than to bury myself into the desk and disappear.

"By the end of school
he yells an answer:
'She should be a pancake.

She has a pancake face'.
It doesn't make sense
until/it does" (Lai 196).

Once again, the words on the page propel my mind to the past. This time, I'm back a few days after the start of eighth grade. Exchanging whispered jokes throughout class, I had befriended the pale, freckled boy that sat beside me in Earth Science. With his witty humor, he managed to make the tedious periods somewhat bearable. That's not what I remember him for, however. I remember him for his mortifying words.

"If I were to rate you, you would be a nine out of ten, but you're Asian so you subtract two. So, you're a seven out of ten." Although a lame attempt at a joke, it was certainly not funny to me. The words became a broken record, repeating themselves over and over, eating me alive and slowly depleting me of all remaining self-esteem. I realized that as long as I was Asian, I would never meet the standards of ideal Western beauty defined by long-legged girls with big eyes, cascading blonde hair, and thin noses. I would never be conventionally pretty, and that was that. I never wanted to talk to the freckled boy again.

I wish that after being taunted for my religion in art class, I didn't feel the need to bear a cross on my neck until seventh grade to pretend I was Christian.

But I did.

I wish that after the comment from the freckled boy, I didn't feel the need to spend months afterwards waking up extra early to coat my face with my mother's makeup.

But I did.

I wish that I didn't feel the need to go home and cry after being called a chink by the boy that I liked.

But I did.

I wish I didn't feel the need to lie for years saying that I was Hawaiian in an attempt to hide my Asian origins.

But I did.

"No one would believe me

but at times
I would choose
wartime in Saigon
over
peacetime in
Alabama" (Lai 195).

Upon reading these lines, I couldn't help but compare myself to Ha. Admitting that for her, peacetime in Alabama, which essentially entailed discrimination from her peers, was at times worse than the horrors of war, validated my own feelings in a way. For me too, it seems as if the smallest, most outwardly insignificant details are the ones that I hold on to. Nevertheless, I couldn't help but think to myself, does it ever get better?

The ending answered my question:

"Not the same,
but not bad
at all" (Lai 234)

Despite the relentless mocking, little Ha eventually achieves tranquility within her new life. *Inside Out and Back Again* manifests the light at the end of the tunnel—that confidence is possible to regain. There is undoubtedly a sort of silent acceptance that young Asian Americans are denied a place in Western popular culture, making it so easy to feel like the only Asian in this world facing discrimination. But this novel gave me first hand evidence of other soldiers in this battle. That knowledge, and especially knowing that many have overcome these same struggles, brings comfort.

I now understand that changing how people think or what they say is not my responsibility, let alone within my power. Instead, it's up to me to recognize my own self-worth. In the end, only I can develop or diminish my sense of self. I must learn to stand unaffected by external judgments. It will take time, but I have hope—hope that I only began to see upon reading this novel. Maybe I don't actually wish that I wasn't Asian. Instead, may I wish for the strength, the courage, and the will to accept myself over time and to one day, to claim victory over my demons of insecurity.

HER

PATRICK WANG

In 9th grade I stared into a
mirror and waged a war with
the boy I saw shattered along
edges of American manhood
sealed off by narrow walls
of conquest and violence
as I reached its pearly gates
other men entered carrying
their lexicons of cruelty
"damn, you fucking killed *her*"
"let's fuck the shit out of *her*"
her has no place in this society
her is a mere game of
smash or pass
"Pass *her*? I'd smash *her*"
in this society men communicate
through clenched teeth
"no homo"
to excuse touch but all I see
are little boys learning to say
"not human"
"I am not human"
"You are not human"
"*her* is not human"
her is a crippled doe
lying lifeless across
man's shoulder
the prize of war

That once broken boy I saw
never entered those
barbed wire gates

the price was too great
I refused to give up
my humanity
he/him/his
masculinity is mine to
define:
"I am human"
"You are human"
"She is human."

BROWN-SKINNED GIRLS

ANUSHKA E.

i will always remember those brown-skinned girls
with beautifully thick blankets of dark hair
the warm dirt under their blackened feet
as the foundation of their playground
from the moment the sun opened its burnt orange eyes
until the innocence of day disappeared
were they compelled to work in a predator's field
they had been recklessly stripped of their volition
for their megaphones were replaced
with brooms and beatings and burdens
their voices became caged prisoners
silent and afraid and tortured
the water they carried above their heads
was a mixture of the polluted streams with their tears
fear was no longer a distant thought
but rather a terrifying countdown
before another lion decided
their ravenous appetite
craved the taste of a helpless creature
those brown-skinned girls
with their petrified expressions
as they heard her scream and struggle
while the predator leaped on his prey

LOOKING FOR JOY

ALAINA DISALVO

CCD was the acronym without a meaning.

I learned today that it stands for Confraternity of Christian Doctrine. No one knew that back then. I doubt anyone knows that now. Catholics aren't big on learning things. Just on making sure others learn them, whether they like it or not.

I'd go every week after school to St. Patrick's Church. I didn't like it very much, but it was essential to my education, as my father insisted. I knew my father wouldn't lie to me.

I never really told him how much I hated going. I didn't want him to be sad. I'd tell my mother. I told her everything. She would smile wide, tell me how wonderful it was going to be the next time, and leave the room. She couldn't look me in the eye afterwards.

I had long hair back then. It fell far past my shoulder blades. My father would have me sit on the floor between his knees as he brushed it back. He would use detangler, he would use conditioner, he would use special rubber bands that were meant to reduce the ache, but I would cry every time. I hated my thick, frizzy hair. I hated that I found comfort when he would brush it, even though it stung.

He'd give me two ponytails, tied so tight that my whole scalp throbbed. Friends would make fun of me for them. I went to him in tears, one day, and asked why I couldn't have one ponytail like all the other kids. He told me that the others were simply jealous. Two ponytails were much better than one. He pretended not to hear when I argued.

"What does Heaven look like?" the CCD teacher asked, on the first day.

Hands shot into the air. I watched. I didn't understand.

Smiling faces, round with the lack of all they had seen, dutifully answered the call: "Rainbows. Clouds. Sugar and joy."

All eyes turned on me.

"What does Heaven look like?" the teacher asked me, expectantly.

I knew what I was meant to say. But my half-formed dreams clouded my already splintered vision. I knew what I thought. It didn't fit what the other kids had said.

The teacher's face began to fall.

"Old men in an oil painting," I proudly proclaimed. "Cracked and yellowed, eyes unfocused, looking for joy from the bottom of their graves. They're very angry, but they're all saints, so it's alright."

The teacher looked away and changed the subject.

I didn't phrase it that way, back then. The words wouldn't fit in my tiny mouth. But I can still see the image in my head, and that's exactly what it was.

I had never realized that God was supposed to be a joyous thing.

When I thought of God, I thought of my father's glare as I lowered the kneeler onto the floor much too loudly. I thought of the rare days that he would force me to go to Church, and how I never saw him open a Bible. I thought of the yellowed piece of paper on my mother's dresser, covered in tally marks of all different colors, reading words that I wouldn't understand for a long time. I thought of the Psalm she would read every single morning but had failed to memorize after more than ten years.

I had a "Read With Me Bible" as a kid. I still have it, somewhere, falling to pieces on my bookshelf. All I remember from that book is King Nebuchadnezzer and the men he failed to burn alive. I loved how complicated his name was- here was someone else who'd never find their name on a keychain. There were some wonderful stories about Jesus in there, too, but it all seemed very far away. I read it the same way I read Percy Jackson, or Harry Potter. It never seemed like something I could relate to.

God was *itchy*. God was too-loud clicks of heels on marble floors, uncomfortably wet kisses from relatives I didn't know, and a faraway force that had never helped me.

God seemed like an old, decrepit man who didn't like me very much. God seemed like the complicated words that my father would use on purpose when talking to me so he'd seem smart when I was confused. So when someone asked me what Heaven was like, that's what I shared.

On my worst nights, when I was about five years old, locked in a room in my father's house with the phone hidden far out of reach, I would pray. I would beg God to bring my mother to save me, beg Him to make me forget about my mother completely so I could learn to love the days I spent with my father. Neither prayer was ever granted.

I hated my First Communion outfit.

I wore a veil. The harsh comb on top of it dug into my scalp with a fury. That veil is the only thing I remember about that day, except for this:

"What did it taste like?" asked an uncle I would stop speaking to in a few years. "The Eucharist?"

I made a face. "Stale, whole-wheat cardboard."

He looked confused.

I missed my Confession.

I had a whole group of kids that were supposed to do it with me. But for some reason- I'd bet my life savings that I had gotten Strep Throat for the tenth time in a year- I missed the Confession ceremony.

The church set up an alternate date for me to show up, alone, with one other child to receive Confession.

The CCD teacher had given us examples of sins to confess. *I kicked my sister while playing soccer* was a popular one. I didn't play soccer. I didn't have a sister. But I'm pretty sure that's what I told the priest, anyway. I reveled in the feeling emanating from his hand placed on my head. It was like an egg cracking on top of my skull, purifying my mind and cleansing my soul. I wonder now how much of that was real.

The priest gave me and the other child stickers after our Confession: saints that matched our birthdays. For November 8, I got St. Stephen. At eight years old, I was sure that this man's name was "steff-en." No one bothered to correct me as I rambled about him being stoned to death. I don't think they were listening.

I mentioned it to the CCD teacher one week, and she regarded me with confusion. There was no St. "Steff-en," she insisted. I must be mistaken. I must've imagined it. I must be wrong, as children so often are.

When I stared at a light for long enough, colored spots would swim in my vision. My father told me the spots were angels. I would stare proudly at the sun for much longer than anyone else I knew, because I thought the angels were protecting my eyes. Blue and green would dance in front of the light, and I would give thanks.

Thank you, I would pray. *Thank you for making me special.*

When I was very young, I sat in a church. It was some gathering of my father's family- I don't remember what. All I do remember is the huge, black spot that danced in front of the altar. I screamed and cried at the sight, frightened in a way that I had never been before. My father allowed me to go outside. He told me that I had seen an archangel. Or a demon. I don't remember which.

My father's cousin was a very spiritual woman. We'd drive all the way up to the Bronx to visit her. I would lose my footing on the steep slopes that held up her apartment building. She would smile at me in her cluttered apartment filled with weeds and skittish cats, and tell me I was special. One day I drew a picture of what I knew my guardian angel must look like. I drew a bunch of vowels and consonants together into what must've been an 18-letter monster, confident that God had put the name of my Guardian Angel into my mind. My father's cousin smiled at me, and I was so proud.

Even then, I felt like the angels were laughing at me.

Religion got worse as I grew.

When I was around ten, I wore a tiny silver cross around my neck, with an even smaller diamond set in the middle. I didn't wear it because I was religious. I wore it because my mother's sister had given it to me.

At a Passover Seder filled with my father's girlfriend's relatives, I clutched it so hard my knuckles turned white.

My father made me take it off before the dinner. "We don't want to flaunt the fact that we're different," he said. "Don't worry. God won't mind."

I had no choice but to leave it behind.

Every other weekend, I'd be in Philadelphia, or upstate New York, or some other place where my father's new family lived. I concentrated on the pulse of my mother's blood flowing through my veins. I wouldn't let myself get sucked into this world of people who didn't know me.

I'd be in silence, no matter where we were. The house. A nursing home. A carnival. A t-ball game. I'd wrap myself up in my own thoughts, sending out a cry to the universe. I would pray for God to send me a boyfriend. A boy who would save me. A boy who would whisk me away from my father and take me to a place where I would be happy. I knew it would happen. I just needed to concentrate as hard as I could. God wouldn't fail me this time.

I'd suck in my belly. I'd stick out my chest. I'd brush my lips with my toothbrush so they'd swell up, try to cross my legs and twirl my hair as coyly as I could. I was never feminine, but I tried so hard to be. If I could get a boy to fall in love with me, I could use him to my advantage. He'd be my ticket out of here.

I think I was twelve when I started doing this.

God never did send me a boyfriend.

When I was older, my father dragged me to a church that we had never visited before. He asked me to get him "a missellette." I had only been to Mass twenty-odd times in ten years, so I had no idea what "a missellette" was. But this did not earn me mercy.

Later that morning, during the Mass, I couldn't stop tears from falling down my face. But I stared resolutely at the altar, even as my father's gaze burned a hole in my temple. I was so proud of myself that day. What a rebellion! I refused to look at him, and never faltered.

I knew that the holiness of churches lied in the respect people gave them. No one dared curse or gossip inside such a holy place. People always spoke in hushed voices, sat silently, and listened to the priest with wonder in their eyes.

If you haven't figured it out by now, I rarely spent time with other children.

The magic spell broke when I started rehearsals for my Confirmation in middle school.

The kids would cackle and scream, cursing and laughing up a storm. They'd roll their eyes at the priest. A boy nicked my phone out of my back pocket when we were standing on line in front of the altar and laughed about it with his friends.

On the day of my Confirmation, the incense stung my eyes so badly that my makeup ran down my face. I sat dutifully in my pew, hands folded in my lap, next to a boy who loved to poke my shoulder and touch my hair without permission. I stared up at Jesus on the Cross. *My God, my God, why have you forsaken me?*

I couldn't feel the magic in the church anymore.

High School was an awakening.

Like they could smell my attraction to girls, the religion teachers doubled down. Every class was an inundation of the horrors of abortion, of dressing provocatively, of having sex before marriage, of even *thinking* about the softness of another girl's lips.

Of course, by that time, I had made my first friends.

Most of them ended up being queer, just like me.

In High School, we'd go to Confession as a group. The religion teachers would hand out papers detailing the sins we might've committed. We had come a very long way from kicking our sisters during soccer practice.

Instead of stressing, instead of feeling guilt crawling up my spine, I giggled with my friends in a pew in the back of the church. We doodled flowers over explanations of the commandments, genderqueer symbols over *Have you had inappropriate thoughts about a peer of the same sex?* We hid the papers in our skirt pockets as the religion teacher walked by, still laughing.

"Are you going to go up to confess?" my friends would ask.

"No," I'd respond.

I thought of my father, aging and balding somewhere out there in the world as my mother sued him for custody. I thought of the psychologist I had sat down with, outlining everything I had ever gone through. I thought of late nights where I'd lie awake, staring at the ceiling, praying to God even though I wasn't sure if He was listening.

"I have nothing to be sorry for," I would say.

I see the church as just a regular old building, now. But I

have found the magic again.

The magic is in the laughter as I clap along with thirty other girls in my school's Gospel Choir, singing our hearts out to God. The magic is in texts I get from my friends at one in the morning, in the small smiles that grace my lips in the darkness. It's in the knowledge that the worst part of my life is over, that I will wake up every morning in my mother's house, and that I will never have to see my father again. It's in the laughter that bubbles up my throat as I sit around the table with my chosen family, my small yet mighty bunch. It's in the connections I forge with other people as I finally grow my own identity.

I still think God is angry with me, sometimes. But I know in my heart that He isn't.

HANDS

LAYA REDDY

We crept through the worn-down shed and leap-frogged
across the baked grass, twigs imprinted on fingers. I bested you

in the race, nothing new, to win grubby, red-crossed palms.
You gripped them until only your nails' pale crescent moons remained.

You cracked my knuckles like Kit Kats, all at once, no mercy,
and asked if it hurt. I said no and asked about your mom

who didn't leave her room anymore. You said she was fine and do
not worry. I pulled hard on your braid, and you snatched up

another finger like it was a glow stick on a rack. We both lied.
Years after, I wondered if the loneliness ever ate you—one bite.

My ring finger was the same as yours and was crooked like yours
and shared rings with yours: class rings, Ring Pops, promise

rings. You promised under the bleachers in fifth grade, remember,
so why would you fit your engagement ring on our finger?

Running in Vienna on cobblestones, trying not to get pitched
off course like my life had, I saw coarse brown strands that could have

belonged to two pigtails from Ohio. My leg muscles pulsed even quicker,
in tandem with my mind, racing forth to yank that familiar hair,

to follow you like I never did before. (We had never been two people.)
Two hands, same ring finger. Suddenly, you were a wrinkled nun.

You were a cynical nurse. You were a fresh-faced barista. You were
a hooded woman in sunglasses, westbound. You were everywhere.

Did it even matter? To each other, we were both lost.

ALL-NIGHTER

MARGAUX EMMANUEL

Your name sounds French
but your bohemian dissatisfaction
mouths the language of quiet, dead alleys
snaking through aisles of
pointillistic women
a fuming cigarette in one hand
a regretted tattoo in the other
standing
at the edge of an embittered balcony
desperately
trying to numb
an undefined pain.

You're an emotional billiard
hanging on to the resin
of the plastic straws
gently swirling
in the *café au laits*
sipped at the windowsill
in an over-large t-shirt
of some punk band you used to like,
hanging on to the melody of
the southern accents
spilling out of the crowds underneath,
hanging on to the awaited surprise of the
honey, I'm home,
crawling up to you from behind
to kiss your neck.

But then
you coughed up the seeds of pain
and let them bloom.
An abruptmascara-dripping

adieu
and now you're here,
sipping a lemonade,
gripping a bouquet of nostalgia.

At least you don't cry as you used to.

ELEGY (GLADIOLUS)

SABRINA GUO

The atrate doesn't understand
the briskly cold embrace
of the cherry blossom trees

as she carries the bundle of gladiolus
and litters them
over Mother's grave—

but she knows too well the prick
from pine needles
as the blood is absorbed

into the chipped cedar limbs, running
through the burning forest of grief—

don't look back now.

The umbrella swung with rain
sticky fingers grasping the handle.

The fog engulfing the tip
of the umbrella:

the lonely light
of a lighthouse
illuminated by the auroras—

you already left.

She remembers like icicles hanging
over glass windows—
when Mother was a biblioklept,

running through aisles

of lemon-scented books,
silver-engraved titles disappearing

with her.
She wonders if she had much to lose—

Mother, return and replace your body
with blue roses.

STRAWBERRY MOON, STRAWBERRY BABY

NATALIE OWEN

salty red-honey sauce, baby-hair curls of chocolate:
what i saw through the window
the night i skinny-dipped and ran
(barefoot heels scraping asphalt at the crosswalk)
to find you at work.
you were backlit.
my skin, with gaping mouth
(goosebumps)
wanting, through the glass,
your cool soft ponytail against my collarbone.
hungry naked stare catching through the window
wealthy women dining, flash of teeth and rings
and your smooth strong brown hands
polishing wine glasses.

things would be different
if we were the last two bodies on earth.

ted bundy and his girlfriend had serial killer
sex.
we watched their fuzzed out whacked out
story
on the couch in your basement
while upstairs, your mom ate celery and chia seeds
(into the night, cold money)
and didn't think to ask
her daughter if she kissed girls.

the moon that night was strawberry.
i remember because i wanted to look,
but you were too afraid she would see us.
we snuck out the bulkhead,

filing-cabinet escape to Narnia,
and i drove your truck barefoot
wrapped in a white blanket
the one with the moth-eaten baby-blue edges
and rusty blood stains
from the time we raced across the train yard at sunset
and had a bloodyfoot picnic.

wrong side of town.
i cat-napped on my front porch beneath the locked door
eyelids fluttering shut on the pink glow moon
at her peak in the grainy sky
curled in my dirty white blanket,
thinking about your skin under my rough thumb
and your sour morning breath at 1 a.m.

caressed by the moon's gentle fingers i slept.
innocent as a waterbirth infant
fresh and wet.
strawberry moon, strawberry baby.

i dreamed that maybe, after all,
we were the last two bodies on earth.

soft bubble dream, dream of a
porch cradle babe beneath blushing orb.

but a spider stepped across my lip
as the sun cracked
(soft-boiled, runny, wet drunk tears)
over the building across the street
and you didn't text me again until a few weeks later
to tell me you weren't in town.
you were, though—
i had seen your shadow polishing glasses
monday nights when i walked by,
arched soft hands rubbing lemon oil cloth,
in the dimly lit restaurant where rich women ate—

but i understood.
my thumb and my tongue argued.
heartbreak tasted different in the daytime
when i saw earthly bodies
but was dreaming of celestial ones,
dancing, tangled, breathing into each other
in the sky, on your couch, on tiptoe tracing outlines.

at night wasn't so bad.
but i found your number in my wallet
the other day while reaching for my subway card
and found metal in the back of my throat,
my throat that had laughed and flirted
and whispered love with you late on a june night.
i felt the weight of my eyes as they had been
looking up at the fat strawberry moon
from my porch as i (baby) dreamed into you.

slipping through the T turnstile i blink—
we are not the last two bodies on earth.

How to Look for Magic in the Stars

Drishika Nadella

Step 1: Choose a location
the abyss of your existential
doom
the comforting recesses
of your terrace;
your mother's begonias
and a pack of chips
to keep you company
(it can get pretty
lonely under
the stars)
and the smell of
salt and nectar and vinegar
hangs in the air

Step 2: Wait for the night
as the sunlight
angles through the trees
the sky, an iridescent mixtape
of blues and reds
try to sneak in
two more chapters of
Jules Verne
before the night bares all

and the stars demand
your unwavering attention

Step 3: Look at the sky
look
for the Galilean contours
for the fireflies that
mimic the uncharted stars
for the Tychoesque speckles
for the wildlife
lurking in the
bespangled veil
bears, dragons, crabs
(you are encouraged
to create your own)
look at the sky
deliberately, shamelessly
for your
apotelesmatic reckoning

Step 4: Discern the magic
decorate the walls
of your soul with
the celestial tapestry
let shooting stars
emanate from your veins
revel in the

nebular dust that has
settled in your blood
let the odds
of your inexplicable existence
in the cosmos
weigh you down

Congratulations, you have found magic in the stars!

CANVAS

TEEN LITERARY JOURNAL

How to Carve
a Jack-o-Lantern

Jyotsna Nair

Step One: Choose the Right Pumpkin

She points to one she claims is perfect.
"How is that different from this?" I snap, holding up the one I'd
picked. It's chilly, the farmer's impatient, and I'm irritated that she
thinks she's better at this.
"This one's still unripe." Sabrina taps it with a finger, with the air
of an expert. "See? (I don't) You'll spend ages scooping the flesh out."
"Fine." I put the pumpkin down. "You win."
"It should be the size of your head." Sabrina picks up her pumpkin.
"That's what Grandpa said."
"Whatever." I hand the farmer ten dollars.
"No."

Sarabeth's mouth formed a perfect circle and her eyes went
impossibly wide. "Why?"

"It's too small." I replied, picking up two pumpkins in my
hands. "Needs to be the size of your head."

"Oh." Sarabeth frowned, and pointed to another one. "How
about that one?"

"Better."

It was the day before Halloween, and we had managed to
arrive at the farmer's market before they'd run out of pumpkins.
Sarabeth had insisted that, since she was a "big girl," she would
pick and make her own lantern. Piles of tangerine—colored orbs
were stacked up around us. Sarabeth was taking ages to choose.

"Hurry up!" I had forgotten to grab a warmer jacket, and the
cold was searching out every uncovered part of my body. The
air was crisp and when I spoke, fog surrounded my mouth like
smoke from a dying cigarette.

"All done!" Sarabeth handed the farmer her money, giving
him a huge grin, showing off the gap between her two incisors.

She bent down, and panted slightly as she picked up her

pumpkin. I noticed that she was wearing Sabrina's old mittens—the ones with silver snowflakes embroidered on them.

The pumpkins slowed me down, but Sarabeth was skipping ahead gaily, singing songs to herself. It was getting colder, and my ears felt numb.

"Baz?"

"Mmhmm?"

Sarabeth looked slightly confused. "Why do we have three pumpkins?"

"Why do you think we do?" I was exhausted after a three hour athletics session, and so the words came out sounding harsher than I'd intended.

She didn't notice. She was too busy puzzling over my question. I waited for her eyes to go wide with realization, and wasn't disappointed.

"Oh!" She gasped. "I get it!" For a second, she looked almost pleased that she'd figured it out. Then she fell silent, and her skipping slowed down to a crawl.

"Yeah." I reached out and squeezed her hand. She looked up, honey-brown eyes glittering with tears. It's been almost a year, but she still hasn't come to terms with it.

I haven't either, really.

Step Two: Scoop Out the Flesh

She's wearing denim overalls, and her blonde hair is bundled into a hat. Apparently, this part requires old clothes because it's extra messy.

She wipes her knife on a cloth before slicing the top of the pumpkin off.

"You have to save it for later." She grabs my hand when I'm about to throw it away. "To cover the lantern with."

"Uh-huh."

Mom doesn't let us use knives to scrape the meat of the pumpkin out. So we use spoons, and later, our hands, tearing away flesh from the skin, digging out seeds and holding them up triumphantly as if they're gold nuggets. Sabrina's overalls, and my shirt, are covered with

orange muck. It's even in our fingernails.
"Baz! Don't eat it!"
Sabrina loves acting like the older one.

Grandpa Tom taught Sabrina how to carve jack-o-lanterns, and she taught me. He would've taught me too, but I'd had the flu at the time. So she did. Like everything that involved her bossing me about, she 'd relished the experience.

I had already scooped the majority of the flesh out, and I paused to wash my hands, which were filthy. Sarabeth was nowhere in sight. Mom was probably helping her out in the kitchen. I should have been helping her, but I was used to *taking* orders from little sisters, not giving them. And it would have felt strange.

Entering the house was like stepping into a sauna. The kitchen was warm, and smelled like cinnamon because Mom had been making doughnuts. It was freezing in the garage. I felt like my fingers had turned into pointy icicles—I'd taken my gloves off. I'd have gone inside, but Sabrina and I had always done this in the garage. She'd always said it was fun to deliberately make a mess.

She had been messy in general. Hair that was more knots and tangles than actual hair, odd shoes and mismatched socks, nails painted every color of the rainbow. Her eyes were blue and green and brown and gold, as if they had been painted several times. I'd use to think that whoever made humans had put in her, a little bit of everything in his toolkit, because there was no other way she could be so . . . *distinctive.* Quirky, even. With regard to everything in her life.

I took my knife again, and scraped out more pumpkin meat. Mom sometimes uses it to make pies, or a special kind of flapjack. Sabrina, for all she loved Halloween, hated eating anything with pumpkins in them.

Sabrina had been the only person in the whole school to belong to every single club. Chess. Soccer. Ballet. Knitting. If there was a problem in her schedule, if there was orchestra the same time as chess, she would run madly across the whole school, popping into each room, staying for maybe ten minutes before dashing off again, coming back because she'd forgotten her bag, and rushing away once more . . .

It was how she had lived. She had journeyed down the road called life like a friendly hurricane. Impacting everyone in her way . . . before suddenly dissipating into air.

This time last year, we'd known that Sabrina wouldn't get a chance to carve a jack-o-lantern again. She had refused to cry over it. Well, she'd cried a *little*—when she was with me, or Dad or Mom—never in front of Sarabeth. *Life is a cycle,* she would say, *and death is just one stage. I'm just moving on a little faster than all of you.*

It had been too fast for me to grasp. She had fallen ill the day after her best friend's birthday party, which was why Mom and Dad assumed it was due to over-excitement and/or hangover symptoms.

It was after her nose had bled for five minutes without stopping that we'd realized something was seriously wrong.

It was after three consecutive visits to the hospital that we realized there was nothing we could do about it.Metastasis had occurred too quickly.

I threw my knife down, sweaty despite the autumn chill. Sabrina had died a week after New Year's Eve, and, ever since then, I had been silently, almost unconsciously, counting down the days to the first Halloween without her. I suddenly wanted to rip apart the paper ghosts and rubber spiders Mom had decorated the house with; throw Sarabeth's witch costume out of the window; hurl every pumpkin in sight into a garbage can.

I hated Halloween for daring to exist without her.

Step Three: Carving

"It should look like it's smirking." She says. " Like it knows something you don't. Like it knows the way to your bedroom, and it's gonna scare you there."

"How do you carve a smirk?" I demand. She smirks.

"Isn't it brilliant?" Sarabeth beamed. Her hair, her face, her clothes—they were covered in flecks of orange. *Looks like someone else inherited the messy gene.* She was holding up a carved

pumpkin, and asked the question in a way that showed she didn't expect an answer to the contrary.

"Sure." I grinned, ruffling her hair. Her pumpkin looked more like a chubby monkey than anything remotely scary, but of course I couldn't tell her that.

Sabrina had always insisted on giving her jack-o-lanterns dimples. I had dimples, one on either cheek, something she'd been absurdly jealous about. If she didn't have them, at least her lanterns did. It was her little quirk. She was Sabrina, and therefore even her jack-o-lanterns had to have something special; something different.

"Haven't you finished making hers yet?" Sarabeth asked.

"Nope." I replied. I had scooped the flesh out, but every time I thought of carving it...it was another reminder that she wasn't there anymore.

Sarabeth looked at me intently, and nodded once, as if she understood. She looked more like Sabrina than I did— they'd both shared the insanely bright, sunshine yellow hair and double-jointed fingers. When Sabrina had died, Sarabeth had refused to let us take her to the mortuary. She had started screaming, in a high-pitched, croaky voice before going limp and eventually succumbing to tears.

An image in my mind of Sarabeth's face, blotchy red and glazed with tear-stains , was shattered when I heard the house phone ringing. I went inside to take the call, after reminding Sarabeth to get extra candles.

It was Grandpa Tom. We chatted for about half an hour before he took a swipe at the subject we'd both been avoiding.

"Are we still at the jack-o-lanterns?" His voice was wheezy, from years of tobacco.

"Yeah."

"Must be weird, without her correcting you every step of the way."

Sabrina loved many things, but she loved correcting me best. *No, Baz! That's not how you do it!* It would have been annoying if she hadn't sounded so *genuinely* troubled by my mistakes. Thirteen years worth of Halloween pictures lay in the family album, encased in cellophane slips. Pictures of every pumpkin she and I had ever carved; of all the costumes we'd worn. Sabrina as a unicorn. Sabrina as a cowboy. Sabrina as a Chinese dragon, a fairy, a ballet dancer . . .

Last year, she had dressed up as . . . a pumpkin. Orange sweater, orange leggings, and a green hat. Hair shortened by chemotherapy, but it was still jaw-length, and even though she didn't have dimples, her smile was *happy*.

"Yeah." I said again. "It is."

Grandpa Tom sighed.

"I won't keep you. Give Sarabeth a kiss from me."

"Sure."

When I came out, Sarabeth was lighting candles. She had already put about eight in her own lantern, and was trying to stick a few in mine. I noticed that someone had finished carving Sabrina's lantern.

"Did you do this?" I asked, pointing at it, trying not to sound accusatory. I knew it couldn't be Sarabeth; it looked too good.

She shook her head, ponytail swinging. "No. I think Dad did. I went in to look for all the candles, and it was done."

"Pretty quick job." I remarked, picking the lantern up to get a better look. I couldn't help feeling resentful. I would have liked to do it myself. Sabrina would have protested, but if she'd had to choose someone to carve her lantern, she'd have picked *me* to do it. I was her jack-o-lantern *protége*, after all.

The pumpkin was the perfect shade of orange. It was the color of the sun at sunset. It had an evil, pointy smirk. I traced my finger along it's skin . . .

When I noticed it, I stopped breathing for a second.

The lantern fell out of my shaking hand. It narrowly escaped destruction by falling onto the grass instead of the concrete. I felt a chill that had nothing to do with the cold creep over me, the way darkness creeps into the day.

"*Baz!!*" Sarabeth exclaimed, crossing her arms and glaring at me. (She sounded uncannily like Sabrina, although I was too dazed to notice). "You could have *broken* it!"

My legs reacted to shock quicker than the rest of my body did. I ran inside the house, and slammed the door shut before sinking to the floor. I pressed a hand to my forehead. My skin felt clammy and wet. My breaths came bursting from my lung in short, ragged gasps.

The image of Sabrina's lantern flooded my mind and burned my eyes.

Smirking, because it knew something I didn't (it *did*! Dad hadn't carved it . . .). A perfect smirk.

Right down to the dimples that had been carved into its cheeks.

HALLOWEEN ...
THE HAUNTED SCRAMS!

Oreo_M

It's cold, breezy outside
        no children playing, they are hidden inside
Lock your doors, stay indoors!
        on this very day, Halloween—it roars.
These very streets you will see
        the spirits of Halloween.
           Hear that rustle, that screeching out there.
    Is it a bird, a tree ... ?
           NO
                It's the haunted screams of

Halloween!
It's cold, breezy, and scary outside.

    If I were you I would be sure to hide.
    No place for children to roam around free,

These very streets of Halloween.
These screams you hear they haunt
  this very day they have come alive
    the spirits are here they have arrived

in search for innocent humans like us, to haunt.

On this very day of Halloween,
        hear the rustling, the haunted screams.
Stay hidden, don't ever be seen
        or you will be for dessert, nice human ice cream.

A QUIET HOUSE

ANNA WENZEL

Swish swish.
A light hum, flitting through the halls like a butterfly.
The shuffle of two barely noticeable footsteps.
The light shining down on the garden outside, filtering in through the murky windows.
A young woman is sweeping the hallway of a quiet, almost abandoned mansion. Everything seems spotless, yet she is again inspecting every hallway to clean specks of dust and dirt. The possible abandoned glass of wine or spectacles. Her hair is pulled up in a tight, neat braid, and her blue dress hasn't a single wrinkle. She looks just as perfect as the rest of the estate, a blush on her skin, her eyelashes fanning across her cheeks.

She glances out the window to the majestic gardens, where no leaves or fallen petals clutter the stone paths. The garden is trimmed in a swirling, endless pattern, and it all looks to be done by one man who moves his way through the garden by sitting on the ground and talking to each individual flower. The maid peeks at him, adoration in her gaze. He was the sole person in the house who smiled at her on her first day.

Moving through the mansion, the sounds are few. The sweeping of her broom echoes down the endless walkways. The paintings of the esteemed aristocrats of the mansion, staring down at the stone floors with angry eyes, are the only things that make the place less lonesome. There is one other person working in the house, a reed-thin cook with strong, bony hands. She is butchering a duck, and many other ducks lay around her with their heads cut off. She is smiling as she does this work, though her smile is violent.

All of these people in this silent house are moving at a pace that contains a barely noticeable sense of urgency. The maid sees a countdown in her head, and it begins to beep louder as the sun shudders, melting into the lake beyond the garden and turning everything a hazy orange.

The corridor lamps flicker to life, causing her to let out a squeak and plaster herself against one of the stone walls, her hair sticking against a painting. She hasn't been working in the house long, and the cook chuckles when she hears the noise coming out of the girl. She still fears this creaking, groaning house that wakes at dusk. It will fade if she manages to last.

Maids come and go easy in this house, the cook knows, because they are always small and pretty. The monsters that lurk the halls tend to like small, pretty things. It's always the shiny objects that catch their attention.

The gardener stands, his body stiff, and walks back to the cottage on the edge of the gardens. For him, there is no use working in the dark. The plants always get trampled, and in the morning he has to deal with their hurt feelings. That is the basics of his job, and after a few years he knows not to come to the plants' aid when they whine at night. The tip of his pinky vanished his first night on the job because he couldn't sleep through the flowers' cries. He learned to buy better earplugs.

The maid peeps out of the window when she hears the slam of the cottage. Her hands begin to shake and she can't seem to control it. She drops the broom in a painful clatter, then scoops it up and runs back to her room and locks the door. She is a lucky one, sweeping right near her own door. She's lucky she even has a lock—some others weren't so fortunate.

She leans against the door and presses her ear against it, a sudden clattering and clamoring beginning to form in the halls.

The maid leaps onto her bed and peers through the tiny window above it. Horseless carriages are rattling up to the main entrance, circling around the fountain in front. Shadowy figures appear at the carriages and open their doors. Each carriage is unique in coloring and decoration. The one closest to her window is midnight black with thick, harsh patterns clawing through the wooden sides and tearing the seams of the back. The wheels are a contrasting silver, and the seat where a driver should be is draped in a gauzy, metallic fabric. The shadow opening the door is wearing a silver top hat.

A grand woman exits the door, her dress swirling around her

like black fog. Her hair is wild, pooling around her shoulders and down to her waist. In a gloved hand she holds a fan decorated with stars that sparkle like the real thing. As she walks to the front door, hand in hand with the top-hat-wearing shadow, other strange folk pile out of the various carriages and gather about the front entrance.

In the hallway, the clamor grows stronger. She rushes back to her door and leans against it again, then wishes she was still at the window when the front doors slam open in their typical style.

The maid has only met her elusive employer on the day she was hired, a few mornings prior, yet she would recognize his booming voice anywhere. He speaks like a man who has seen many things but still zests for more thrills. Her toes tingle as his voice ricochets off the walls and filters into her room. She can imagine him addressing the guests at the front door, though she can't understand his words.

In the kitchen, the cook yanks out food and shoves in the ducks. Outlines of people swarm around her, helping to plate all of the appetizers. She whispers out orders to them as a haunting band shuffles into place in the great room, their bows ripe with the fire of unshed songs. Her foot almost taps along as a familiar beat strikes the stone floors.

The maid feels a pull in the tips of her fingers as cheers begin to go off in the main foyer. Her hands are shifting without her asking, grabbing for the metal knob of her door. It starts to rattle the moment her skin touches the bronze, shaking in time with the pounding music below.

With a gasp, the door flings open and she is pulled into the hallway. Suddenly her hands are her own and she is able to cover her mouth in shock. Tall, ghoulish figures are flickering with the lights and bending around her as they pass down the halls. They are filling up as much space as they can, the tips of their hats reaching the ceilings.

She shuffles through the shifting specters toward the double staircase at the end of the hall. It leads into the opulent main foyer, where the maid sees her employer standing next to the door of the great room. His hat is tipped down so she can't make out his face, but the silver pocket watch that he twirls in between his fingers gives his identity away. He did the same gesture when she first met him. It had comforted her in her anxiety. Now, though, as she stares at his hand, the shapes of him start to shimmer and wave and she isn't quite sure what she's watching anymore.

The fancy guests who had flooded the main entry are now dancing around the great room, their joyful steps hitting the floor as the skeletal quartet at the back of the room leads them in a song.

The maid takes a look at the very long faces of the guests, and the way their teeth glint too sharp in the lowering sun, and makes a beeline for the kitchen. The head cook had never paid her much mind, but she couldn't go back to her room when she wasn't able to trust her own hands.

She tumbles into the swinging kitchen doors as shadows slip by her, their forms plastered against the gold-tinged walls. The head cook is standing at her metal work table, the blood of many ducks sticking to her fingers as she waves them about, directing her helpers. The maid has never heard the cook speak before, save for a polite you're welcome, but now her voice echoes through the room in tiny whispers, somehow rising above the din of the party-goers and somehow barely heard at all.

Sizzles of duck fat and pots of soup fill the air, and the maid is hit with the sweet scent of cucumber and mint. Though her nose tingles, she heads straight for the cook. The cook has noticed the maid now and her eyes are wide. Her mouth pulls into a thin line as the maid pauses in front of her and explains the situation. The cook says in her whispery tone to *leave and return to your room if you want to stay alive*. The maid takes the warning.

As she rushes for the stairs a hand—or maybe a claw— wraps around her wrist and pulls her to the great room.

Her panic steals her voice away and she tugs as hard as she can. She looks at her capturer and sees it to be the grand woman from the front entrance. Her eyes are thinned and her smile is wicked, and when the maid looks at her hand again she indeed sees sharp talons.

A bubble of nausea hits her and she can't help but wonder

if she missed something in the fine print when she saw the help-for-hire ad in the paper.

Her employer is no longer standing by the door of the great room when she enters. She's glad, because to handle his disappointed gaze with the sensory overload she already feels would be too much.

The great room is abuzz with dancing and cheers and tipping champagne flutes and loud music. The maid feels shivers run up her spine as her ears focus on the music. It is bass-heavy and shrill at the same time, the melody almost jarringly overtop. The guests look more fiendish as they dance, their faces jovial and sinister at the same time.

She is spun about, her hands now put in various dance partners wearing over-the-top magical clothes and shoes that shine against the sparkling tile floors too well. The usual soft gold curtains that reach the high ceilings have been replaced with heavy black ones that pool at the floor and highlight the glow of the almost-prominent moon. Above the musicians, away from the windows, is a jutting terrace with no door or stairway leading to it. A massive velvet throne sits upon it, looking down across the room. The maid can almost feel the chair under her fingers because there is one just like it in the dining hall. The velvet is exquisite in its softness, and no touch leaves a mark. In the chair is her employer, and he is staring right at her.

His eyes sparkle in the blur of the room, in the blur of his own face. Though the maid would have called him handsome at meeting, her employer now seems to have a smile too wide, teeth too long, and his eyes look like bottomless pools, even from across the room. His crooked and tangled-looking hand is still twirling the pocket watch, the silver chain so long it keeps brushing against his shiny shoes.

Out of the blur that emanates about him is another hand, though it is slimmer and sharper. It beckons for her to come forward.

In a trance-like state she does, the same feeling from when she had opened the door without her own consent hitting her again.

The maid begins to walk toward the terrace with jelly-filled steps, unsure of why but sure that she must, when something grabs her wrist once more. Everything around her seems to slow as she turns and sees the gardener, his soft, very human hand against her.

The sounds around her dim as she is pulled out of the great room and up the stairs and down the hall and back to her simple little room.

Everything is so quiet and the moon is calming in its rays as it rains on the unlit, empty hallway.

She turns around to thank the gardener, but he is already gone, the kind lines of his smile in her memory the only linger left.

The maid bars her door shut and knots up her hands so she can open no more doors for the night.

She survives the night.

The maid will never see the gardener again.

THE HOARDER

LITA GI

There is a lovely restaurant that lies on the corner of Tacy Street. The fire-engine red walls with golden, swooping letters draws the attention of all hungry folk in the city, beckoning toward the striped diner chairs and bow ties within. Plopped on top of this restaurant, much like a tier of a well-iced cake, sits a pine-brick apartment lined in oil-black eaves. The restaurant buzzed with eager guests and savory aromas. The apartment told a much different story.

The glow of morning sun drowned, struggling to breach the fingerprint-crusted windows. The sill was strewn with corpse-less insect wings and disjointed spider legs from critters who snuck across the fly screen and promptly dropped dead. Particles of dust skimmed in the dim shaft of murky light, drifting like a film of mildew on gutter-side rainwater.

Thick woven rugs scattered the apartment floor, muffling the distant city bustle that wafted through the cracks in the chocolate-painted floorboards and bled with the clatter of silver kitchen tools below. Inside the apartment, however, silence hung its ancient tapestry.

A patchwork of Frankenstein wallpapers lathered the drywall, showcasing a collection of strange frames featuring parchments of scrawled notes and sketches from various yard-sales and flea markets. A ramshackle bookcase held an assortment of pamphlets and brochures, stolen from seminars or tour guides.

Bric-a-brac scrambled over any available surface, cascading onto the floor. Mason jars caked in dried substances, spools of untouched thread, melted candles whose twisted wicks could barely recall the last time they were graced with a flame, crispy remains of once-green leaves, palm-sized pewter figurines, bowls of wooden, paint-chipped beads—

Despite these tokens of traveling in the outside world, one

would never consider Nickolas Plutt anything but a hermit. One would never consider anything of Nickolas Plutt at all.

* * *

"Nick?" Eloise called, her voice an octave higher than normal. Perhaps out of instinct or concern, she sang in the taming voice parents save for children. Her keys chimed as she pushed her way through the curios and into the apartment. She plopped her sagging purse and a brown bag of groceries onto a dry portion of the kitchen island directly adjacent to the door. "I got more pamphlets for ya, bud."

A dark shadow flickered in the bedroom doorway. Eloise noticed it immediately. "Yeah, buddy, here. I know you like them," she coaxed, waving the bright papers at an arm's length as if she were offering treats to a bashful forest animal.

The shadow did not move.

Eloise exhaled. "Fine. I'll leave them here." She dropped the pamphlets on the counter, then proceeded to fish her hand into her purse, fumbling through it blindly like a child and a bag of Halloween candies.

"Is he gone?" a corn-husk voice rasped.

Eloise jerked her head up to the bedroom doorway.

A half-moon face colored like curdling milk lay partially covered by the doorway. An ash-gray iris, sewn into a yellow-tinted eye by strands of spindly blood-ink veins, bore into her.

"There you are," Eloise said, returning to her purse. "Is who gone?"

Nickolas parted his thin lips, his tongue a slab of sandpaper. "Caleb Hart."

Eloise grinned as she pulled her bag inside-out, spilling her items onto the counter. She flicked her ring finger at him as she searched through her contents, showing her wedding ring. "No, honey. We're still together."

Nick receded into the bedroom, overcome by the shadow.

"Aha, found it." Eloise looked up at the shadow and sighed.

"Look, Nick, we had one fight months ago, but we're over it. Husbands and wives stay together. We're not leaving the restaurant any time soon." She pulled an envelope from her purse. "Also, I dropped by to give you these."

The eye returned to peek at her hand.

"I paid."

"We've talked about this, sweetie. You get new bills every month. You need to pay them every time or my hubby will have to kick you out."

Nickolas snapped back behind the door. Eloise cringed.

"Right, I'm sorry, you don't like it when I say that," she said. "Caleb will have to kick you out, is what I meant."

Nickolas grumbled. Begrudgingly, he outstretched his pasty, gray-haired hand.

Eloise leaned against the refrigerator while Nickolas fiddled with the letter. She noticed an old photograph tacked onto the cluttered fridge. She pulled it off and held it up to the light, gasping in excitement. A younger Eloise beamed to the camera in nursing scrubs, leaning over the wheelchair of an elderly gentleman.

"Wow, I completely forgot about this picture!" she exclaimed, bubbling over like a boiling pot. "You still have this from your ... visit?"

Nickolas said nothing.

"Well, alright. I think I'm done here." Eloise kept her voice at the sing-song, joyful pitch as she scooped her belongings into her purse. "I have to go back down to work. See you next week, alright?"

Nickolas occupied himself with the envelope, running his cracked fingernails along the edges. Eloise slung her bag onto her shoulder, preparing to leave. Quite suddenly, a fat blur of mahogany brown launched itself onto the kitchen counter. Startled, Eloise yelped.

"Oh, Nick, what is that?"

His attention remained on the envelope. "Cat."

"How long have you been here, little fella?" Eloise cooed, tentatively stroking the mangled hair of the tabby. "You are just the cutest thing!"

Nickolas now shifted his gaze. He peered from his cloudy haze as Eloise stroked the cat.

"You know what," Eloise reasoned with the tabby, "I could just eat you right up."

Nickolas stared, his eyes in an unfiltered focus.

Reluctantly, Eloise pulled herself away. "Alright. For real now, I have to go. See you soon, Nick." With a brighter smile, she twiddled her fingers at the cat. "Bye, now, kitty!"

As Eloise shut the door behind her, Nickolas stood in his gargoyle state at the doorway. For the first time in months, he had decided to open his cutlery drawer.

* * *

Nickolas could recognize Eloise's footprints out in the corridor.

"Ni-ick," she sang, her fingers drumming the door, "can I come in?"

He remained silent. Eloise took it as a confirmation. Her keys rattled in the doorknob and she entered, the door opening more easily since her last trinket-clearing visit.

"Jeez, why is it so dark?" Her hand slapped at the wall until it connected with a light switch. The lightbulb danced between on and off before deciding to fulfill its purpose.

Nickolas' spirit-like presence hung directly in front of Eloise. She jolted, alarmed.

"Do you usually stand in the dark, right in the doorway?" Predictably, he didn't answer.

"I think I dropped my wallet in here earlier today. Mind if I look?"

Nickolas shuffled to the side, allowing her to pass. She approached the kitchen island but stopped in her tracks. "What's this?" she asked.

The bag of groceries and the pamphlets had been pushed to the corner of the island. A bowl of steaming meat stew lay on the counter, a stool drawn up to it. A dust-covered emerald bottle held a withered daisy, the petals disintegrating.

"Oh, did you cook this for me?" Eloise exclaimed, giggling as she sat down. "That's very sweet of you, Nick."

"Is Caleb gone?" he asked. He didn't sit. He stood across from her, watching as she began her meal.

"No, honey. Like I said before, we're staying together." She ate quickly while she spoke, cramming stew between her words. "We're at a good spot right now; the restaurant is doing great, we're finally decorating our apartment, we're planning a vacation for the break . . . yeah, sweetie, I don't think Caleb is leaving any time soon."

Eloise was about halfway done with her stew before her chewing slowed. Her grin faltered. She let the meat settle on her tongue, her thin eyebrows scrunching. Nickolas leaned in closer, observing.

"What—what is this? Is it pork? It's... strange."

Nick stared at Eloise as she prodded her food, noticing that several chunks of meat were not entirely cooked.

"Y-You know what? I should probably get my wallet and leave. Oh, let me see that little cat of yours!" Eloise slid off her stool and wandered the cramped apartment. "Where is he?"

"There."

"Hmm?"

Nickolas met her look. His pale-moon face remained stoic marble. "There."

"What do you mean, Nick?" Unsettling fingers whispered over Eloise's back. Her voice wavered, her eyes buzzing around the room. "Where's the cat?"

Nickolas pointedly turned to the bowl of stew, and Eloise's gaze followed.

"Oh God," she wailed, her hands springing to her throat.

"Oh, Lord!"

Her stomach growled, unsettled. Eloise tried to rush to the kitchen sink, but Nick stood in her way. Too agitated to sidestep the tall figure, she spun around to the mess of a lounge room, but books and shoes and teacups and coat hangers swallowed her path and she buckled over, retching.

"Is Caleb gone?" Nickolas asked, his composure that of a marble statue.

Eloise moaned, hands and knees on the floor. "Nickolas!" Her chest heaving in cycles, she poured out her insides, her voice strangling.

Nickolas blinked. He took a tentative step backward.

Eloise howled again, her throat raw from vomiting and screaming. "Oh my God!"

Nickolas drew a shaky breath. "Hush. Hush now."

"You're insane!" Panting, her eyes caught the mess on the floor and she gagged once more.

"Hush!" Nickolas whispered. He rocked back and forth on the balls of his feet, his hands wavering uncertainly.

Footsteps from a stranger echoed in the hallway, drawn to Eloise's noise. Nickolas hesitated, hovering over Eloise, his silhouette blocking the single lightbulb. Eloise sobbed, clutching at her neck on the ground.

"Hush!"

She did not.

Nickolas grasped a random object from the nearest table: a hammer.

With one swing, Eloise stopped shrieking.

* * *

Caleb Hart kept himself awake all night, waiting for his wife. He figured she probably fell asleep in the restaurant at Tacy Street, as she was inclined to do when she waited for the restaurant to pack up.

When Caleb opened the kitchen for the day, he did not find his wife poured over some table, dozing.

He did, however, discover an assortment of freshly cut meat in the freezer.

EMMYLOU, OR THE DECISION

R. M. LAWLER

There comes a point in everyone's life when a change comes about quite suddenly that serves as the catalyst for the rest of their mortal life—whether it be the beginning or end of everything remaining to be seen. From this genesis, spreading like the disturbed waves of an unsettled lake, the whole of a person's life is formed. The substance becomes nearly tangible in its absolute authority. This came to be the case for a Miss Emmylou Harris of number 10 Ashton Drive.

As ominous as the earlier skies had seemed in the bitter cold of the blurry morning, the day bloomed into the wonderfully crisp fall day that happened rather seldom in the quiet college town. A refreshing breeze blew out from the craggy shoreline, a hint of salt and sunlight on its breath. It was into this wind that Emmylou stepped out, having just finished hearing a class lecture on the importance of agrarian economics in the nineteenth century. She strode out into the wonderful glory of the day and decided upon taking the long route from the university to her apartment. The wind whipped the gossamer gold of her hair before, quite suddenly and vehemently, it yanked the wool-knit cap from her head. She chased the bright red of the cap in dismay, struggling to catch up to its fleeing crimson hue.

Suddenly, just as her fingers were coming close, close, closer to her lovely knit cap, another hand abruptly grabbed it from the air. And before her feet could stop, she charged straight forward into the body of her hat's captor. Luckily, neither person fell. Standing before her was a tall boy (man?) of about her own age. He offered the hat to her.

"I believe this is yours," he muttered stiffly before promptly handing it to her.

"Thank you! I appreciate it." After a quick smile, she started in again on her path, having quite a bit of research to work on. As she trundled on, suddenly a pair of dirty brown boots came into view beside her. Someone was catching up to her, and quite easily at that.

He cleared his throat before grinning sideways at her and saying, "What's my favorite girl up to?" before placing a palm over his heart.

Oh, good God, she thought. Turning to him, barely refraining herself from an eyeroll, she exclaimed in an unnaturally high falsetto voice, "Why, talking to an incredible imbecile!"

The boy choked before covering it with a cough. "Jesus, Em. That tongue of yours is still as sharp as ever. It truly cuts, you know—see look; I think I'm bleeding!"

She laughed and glanced at him with a sharp smirk.

"If only it would bleed quicker . . . I'm becoming rather bored of your dramatics."

He pressed a hand to his cheek and sighed heavily, "Your words wound me dreadfully. I may not survive this. Unless, of course, you come do research with me."

She fixed him with a look before smiling steadily and uttering, "Well, I'm only saying yes because I had to do research anyways." And with that, they set off for the large stacks of the university library.

To him, Emmylou Harris was always *the girl*. She was divinity in human form and was greater than all the others who had come before. He jealously watched her in his tortured mind's eye because she was the ultimate trifle to be won. Day in and day out, he plotted and planned to make her his, to win over that tempestuous creature. The first time he had every laid his eyes upon her, he had seen her big, dark eyes and cutting smirk; he was utterly intrigued. After he heard her argue with the professor in class and win, he was besotted. And after seeing her lead an intramural team to victory, he was obsessed. Quickly, he joined activities adjacent to hers and sat in decent proximity to her in class. Soon, he started carefully learning all her classes and her daily habits, from her club meetings to her outdoor excursions. Then he began to follow her. Once he even had the courage to accidentally run into her and save her hat; they even exchanged a few words. This was all about to change, though, because he was going to truly meet her, while she was taking her usual path home. And this time, she would become his.

When she did not appear upon the path; however, his devastation was crushing, exacerbated by the fact that he had rescued her hat not an hour beforehand. He lashed out at a few rocks in rage before quickly calming himself. There was no use getting so worked up over the girl, he reasoned. He could just try again tomorrow. With that thought firmly in place, he walked home in complete agitation and anticipation for the events to come.

All night long, he drank and drank in sadness and anger, quiet grief in being denied what was rightfully his. Then his impaired mind firmly decided, "To hell with it all!" With the vodka and whiskey sloshing around inside his stomach and injecting itself into his bloodstream, he decided to drive out to the girl's home, just to have a glance. As his car trundled along, he could not help occasionally swerving into the next lane or going through stop signs. When a siren pierced the air of his drunken reverie, he jerked sharply to the left. Before long, his car was pulled over, and he was having to explain (slowly and patiently) that he was just visiting a friend to the irrational officer. He sighed in obvious contempt when he was informed that he had to do a breathalyzer test—that was until he was placed in handcuffs outside the car. He became belligerent at having been thwarted yet again and started to kick and contort his body forcefully. As he was being pushed into the backseat, his heart ratcheted up in tension as he watched a newly arrived officer opening the trunk of the car. When he heard the exclamations of shock, he slowly melded into the seats in utter defeat. It was over.

The morning rose bright and clear. Emmylou rose from bed and went through her normal routine: showering, having a quick breakfast of fruit and yogurt, brushing her teeth, and then leaving for her 9:30 a.m. class. As she walked along the tree-lined path to her destination, she took in the gorgeous blue sky broken up by the thickets of fiery red leaves. Lost in a reverie of what would be discussed in class, she was suddenly jarred by running footsteps and a loud voice, shouting, "Wait up, Em!"

She turned to see her friend crash towards her on his damnably long legs and could not help but smile at the scene before her. As they started to stroll towards class together, he said, rather secretively, "Guess what?"

Raising an eyebrow, her interest only the slightest bit piqued, she offered an obligatory "What?" while shrugging her shoulders.

"Well," he started, before adjusting the worn leather satchel on his shoulder. "You know that guy in our history class . . . Edward? Or maybe Ethan?"

She thought for a moment. "I think so! The quiet one . . . with longish hair?

"Yeah, that's the one."

"Well, what about him?" she rolled her hand, motioning him to continue.

"He just got busted for a DUI. Then when the cops searched his car, they found a shitload of stuff."

Her eyes widened in surprise before glancing up at her friend. "Really? That kind of surprises me, considering how quiet he is. It seems difficult to do business if no one knows you're selling."

"That's the thing though—he definitely wasn't selling. What they found wasn't hardcore drugs either. People have been saying different things, but it seems like it was a combination of pot and a weird collection of things: a hunting knife, twist ties, a tarp. Honestly, serious serial killer type shit."

A beat of silence passed before she said, "Well shit, man. That's quite the way to perpetuate a stereotype. How long could he be in for? After all, there's nothing definitively wrong with owning that stuff. It's a bit odd to have in your car, yeah," she added shrugging.

"Apparently, he gave the cops some weird vibes, especially considering that girl who went missing about a year and a half ago. Nothing's for sure yet, but rumor has it that the police are getting a warrant for his residence to see what else they can find."

Emmylou shivered and pulled her coat tighter around herself, "Jesus! I feel like I just stepped into a cheesy teen horror movie!" And on that note, they headed off to class.

Little did Emmylou know, as she sat in class, listening to a lecture and tapping her pencil on her chin, that the police had begun their investigation of a certain apartment. Inside, they found exactly what they were looking for . . . and then something more.

Charles A. Surrey, a newly appointed junior officer, was looking through the bedroom—which was a dark, heady-scented place—as a part of his first official assignment when he stumbled upon a small walk-in closet. The door was painted the same ghastly maroon as the wall and was missing its handle. What he found inside, though, was far more disturbing than any horrendous shade of red.

The walls were covered with hundreds of photos—both grainy and brilliantly clear—that overlapped each other in a nonsensical pattern. Every single photo was of the exact same girl. A girl with golden hair whose face usually held a lopsided smirk. As he looked around the small space, he felt slightly sick. Not only were there photos, but there were also scraps of paper covered in slanted handwriting, empty water bottles and stained coffee cups, tattered girls clothing, both student and city newspaper clippings about the girl, used Band-Aids, tissues. And all of it was used to draw attention to a name scrawled onto the wall, in what appeared to be painstaking fashion:

EMMYLOU.

Charles A. Surrey laughed hoarsely. This whole operation had started as a minor drug search and curiosity about some items found in the suspect's car, but had turned into something much, much darker. He turned and left the disturbing shrine, returning only after he had procured his supervisor.

As Emmylou walked along the craggy shore on a cloudy, windswept day, her thoughts turned as they often had in recent months, to troubled contemplation. Ever since she had heard about the apartment bust, about the shrine dedicated to her, she had started to have a newfound appreciation for that fatefully gorgeous fall day. She thanked God, the universe, herself—anything and everything—that she had made that fortuitous decision to do research and then take the long route home instead of her usual one. After all, had she not gone the way she did, she may very well not be here to contemplate anything at all. She had no idea of what would have happened to her if she had gone on her usual journey. With weeks of considerable thought to support her, she resolved that she did not wish, even out of mere curiosity, to know what would have occurred on that wretched day. And so, she continued on the rocky coastline, enjoying both the serenity and fear that comes from being so fragilely bound to this mortal world.

ERASURE

MAYA EPSTEIN

Five hundred and eighty miles away, Lucy Hayden disappeared from the picture frames and her name belonged to no one. Before that, a bell above the door had jangled lazily as he exited, a wave of red dust rushing to the place a welcome mat ought to have been. He had stood outside, holding the door ajar with the battered toe of his boot. For late October, the heat was oppressive, the sun was blinding, fat and buttery, and yet, he felt lighter than he'd ever been before. Inside the gas station, the dust billowed about for a moment, a sort of rust-colored swirl beneath the fluorescent lights. Jude had looked back inside. All was as it should have been—aisles full of SPAM and too- sweet gummies; crushed bags of chips filled halfway with air; cans of pop behind fogged refrigerator doors. Everything, apart from the still-settling dust, was very still. Everything, apart from his racing mind, was very calm. He shifted his boot, letting the door shut properly, and pressed his hands and nose against the windows. Behind him, the rows of overripe corn waved in a nonexistent breeze. He couldn't remember why he had come here. He couldn't remember what he had done.

Before that, everything had gone dark.

Before that, he had been crouched in the gas station's grimy bathroom, sitting on the toilet seat, his head in his hands. The girl and her notebook had been standing across from him. Her back had been pressed to some kind of dispenser (for what— sanitary things, temporary tattoos— he couldn't really tell), the cherry from her lollipop dripping from the end of the paper stick. The room had been far too cramped, and his throat was tight and dry, but he had a sneaking suspicion that his pounding heart had nothing to do with the claustrophobic space. She began to erase her drawing, slowly, steadily. She was humming something, something that sounded like a children's rhyme, and she seemed to have forgotten how to blink. Rubber debris mixed with the sticky-sweet red syrup pooling on the ground. "Lucy Hayden will be erased by morning," said the girl.

"From me?" he'd asked. His voice was wavering, and his mind was racing, and maybe this wasn't such a good idea after all. The girl smirked, and when she spoke again, he saw lip-gloss smeared on her teeth.

"You'll see."

Before that, the girl had drawn Lucy Hayden in her notebook. The girl had asked what color her eyes were when the sun hits them just right. He had said green, pinyon pine green, green like the roadtrips they'd taken in his old pickup. She had brought a magnifying glass to scorch marshmallows. She'd said this was a much safer way to do s'mores, because only you can put an end to forest fires. And he'd been confused because when he was small, all Jude had burned with magnifying glasses were ants, but then, he thought, of course Lucy Hayden didn't burn ants. She was Lucy. The girl asked him what Lucy Hayden smelled like, and he'd said blueberry pie, because that is what he'd ordered the night they met. Before that, the girl had asked if Jude loved Lucy. He had cried. She had handed him a square of toilet paper from the gas station bathroom, her x-ray eyes glittering.

Before that, Jude had stumbled into the gas station, his boots red with dust. He couldn't really see, partly because he hadn't slept in two nights, partly because he was surviving more so than living, which put sight on the back burner. He rushed passed the SPAM and too-sweet gummies, crushed bags of chips filled halfway with air, cans of pop behind fogged refrigerator doors. He was hungry, but not for something so simple as being full, or so trivial as food. His hunger was for emptiness. Jude walked to the counter, where a cashier, a girl, sat on a stool in front of a box fan. It blew her hair wild, and her eyes were closed, and there was a gallon of whole milk with a pink straw in front of her. Jude tapped her on the shoulder. The girl turned the fan off, her eyes still closed, a small smile curling her lips. "What's her name?" the girl had asked. Jude blinked. It was strange to be spoken to by someone, face to face, and yet unable to see their eyes. He wished she'd open them.

"Whose name?" he had responded, cautiously.

"Hers. Say her name."

Jude blinked again, and did not answer. The girl's eyes remained closed. Her smile deepened, curling into a smirk, a plastic, bubblegum-pink smirk, and Jude felt a spark of annoyance. He looked at her for a few moments longer before answering, "Lucy. Lucy Hayden."

The girl's eyes snapped open, and Jude, subconsciously, had taken a step back. Now they were open, Jude wished they'd close. Her eyes were piercing blue, icy, a peculiar shade that made them look unfocused, as if they were drifting to a place just passed his left ear. He felt as though the girl could see right through him: through his clothes, through his skin and webs of veins, through the walls he'd built and broken, to the cytoplasms and nuclei.

After that, he'd rambled, "Are you the one? They said, back in town, you could help me, so I drove two days to get here. They called you a witch. Are you a witch? They said you could help me—" Here, he had gulped, "Forget."

And she had responded, mockingly, taking a big swig of milk and unwrapping a cherry lolly. "I am to you whatever you wish me to be." She had stood then, the sweaty skin of her thighs unpeeling from the red leather stool, and walked towards the gas station bathroom. She looked back at Jude, her impossible eyes oddly bright. "Come," she said.

Before that, Jude Holland drove two days and two nights through the autumn dust, his throat parched and his skin cracking, his boots the only sturdy thing about him, to a gas station in the middle of a cornfield, where it was rumored a girl could help him forget. And two days before that, Lucy Hayden had given him a reason to drive two days and two nights to a gas station, in the middle of a cornfield, where it was rumored a girl could help him forget.

Not So Dark Anymore?!

RUSUDAN JANJALASHVILI

PROLOGUE

Mysteries whisper in the peak of the night,
With the shadows dancing to the edges of sight.
Dead darkness murmurs the secret uncanny,
And marblish phantoms rise in wild sway.
These doomed dark tears mutter the unsaid
And dreams start flourishing in the wildest way . . .
Light of sun draws back in the kingdom of black,
The bittersweet darkness is calling me within!
Gazing into the mirrors of soul in reflection of mine,
I'll say: Drenched in dark ink will thy erelong be,
Letting black curtains clash upon thee!

CHAPTER I
A NEW NEIGHBOUR (?)

"It's not going to be so dark in the house next door anymore"I heard my mum's high-pitched, lovely voice, as sweet as any child thinks of her mother, when I was having an afternoon rest on the sofa, as pleasing as hiding under warm, woolen blankets with a detective book in rainy weather. Still being on the boundary of the consciousness and the dream world—mostly still behind *the wall of sleep*, I realized I had nodded off . . .

"There's a new neighbour coming in,'' she continued, and *after* those words were said, I darted back into reality.

I hardly used to speak when I had just woken up. So, I kept my dazed thoughts to myself—rather sad ones because my best friend, Maeve, who used to live in that house with her family, seemed to have left the house next door once and for all . . . The house was not going to be so dark anymore. I could feel a slight spark of thrill and excitement in my little, naughtily beating heart because of such news. I was a great lover of mysteries, after all. "Hopefully, I will get to see him/her (or even them—perhaps) on my way to school tomorrow . . . or back" I thought to myself and smiled cozily, like a cat stretching by a crackling fireplace, just having caught a sweet prey. Suspense satisfied me, although it was a little thing—it was still unknown, wasn't it?

Little did I know of those bizzare events that were just about to take place . . .

* * *

Needless to say, I looked with a pair of my investigative, large green mirrors of the soul quite closely to the house next door on my short, yet still exhausting way to school next day. I could see no sign of any commitment—usual for just moving into a new house. Not even on my way back.

Not on the following day as well.

Not even on the next day.

For weeks, I found myself unable to catch a glimpse of him, her, or even them.

Nothing. I never saw my mysterious neighbor—they never left the unique coziness of "home, sweet home." I never caught a stranger stepping their stranger foot outside the wooden porch or even observing the surroundings from the square-shaped, cute white windows in front of my bedroom from which Maeve loved so much to jump from—then climb up to my window and play with me when we were supposed to study instead—I missed Maeve. Or it would be better to say that I missed my childhood memories with her. I could hear her happy laughter in my head whenever I took glimpse of those golden brown curtains behind the white windows which now seemed to be left untouched.

I was trying to keep my eyes wide open with childish curiosity whilst I was spending time in the garden as well, looking after my adorable, snow white and crimson red roses on which the warm sun was melting in the golden August evenings, but in vain—I never saw a glimpse of the inhabitant of the house next door . . .

Until a strange occurrence one day—I was in my bedroom, as usual, sitting in a rocking wooden armchair with the diary on my knees, the setting sun kissing my cheekbones warmly, with my reflections pleasantly bewildered, when I felt an unfamiliar but urgently realizable feeling of . . .

Being watched.

I instantly looked up and with a corner of my eye, I caught a glimpse of the golden brown curtain being slightly dragged and a dark silhouette quickly crossing the room in the house next door. In a blink of an eye, it happened, but I could swear I had not nodded off. I felt a peculiar consciousness existing around me. A sinister chill ran down my spine.

The truth was, my ears did not need as strong mobilization as my eyes. The reason why I was so eager to see what our neighbor looked like, was a simple curiosity of who was the source of those noises coming from the house next door, who was causing the sounds of screeching, walking, whispering, and sometimes even laughing . . .

I was sure that those noises were coming from that house. I was as sure of it as I was about that fact that I was not dreaming. But since no one else at home seemed suspicious about these occurrences, I did what any other person would do to avoid misunderstandings and being perceived as crazy—I turned a blind eye to it. As a normal child.

I should not have done that. If only I had said something— to mama, to papa, to . . . anyone.

Chapter 2
Run! Run! Run!

For my life, I have to run. I have no idea what the "thing" I'm running from looks like, I am just unconsciously aware of that severe truth that I am still desperately trying to avoid—it's the neighbor from the house next door! I just simply know that the only way of my survival lies in escaping. The primal impulses, existing from the dawn of time, would definitely burst their lungs (if they had any), from screaming that one and only word in my head over and over again:

"*Run! Run! Run!*"

Pitch darkness has almost fully set in. Only a few rays of the golden, naughty sunlight manage to break into the blackness and find their way to my sore body. Primal fear of the unknown has conquered my core, my feet, eyes, hands —every inch of my body. I can see only a few reflections—like images in my head, which do not match what I see by the greenish world between my eyelashes—in my mind, I see a strange swamp, surrounded by a hill on which there is a . . . is that a . . . mirror ?!

But with my eyes, all I can see is a strange piles of high stone walls, similar to the construction of dark labyrinth, covered in mud and dark green epiphytes. The smell of bitter humidity barely makes me breathe . . .

"Run, run, run!"

I can hear a sinister laughter coming from behind my very own back, I feel like my heart is about to break into pieces from an abnormal fear, oh my god, I have to run, but to where? Where the hell am I??? Oh, God, I don't want to . . . die!

But if I want to see my mama again, my lovely white and crimson roses being kissed by the sunshine, the beauty of the setting sun in the delightful summer evening, I must not look back! I am not ready for what I am going to see, I just have to move my legs but why on earth are they slowing down like they are being tied up . . .

But, to much more horror to myself, as if the terrible feelings of I am sensing so far are not enough, out of the blue I already realize that . . .

I had already been here before. Not a long time before, literally just a few moments ago . . .

I am running in the same circle!

* * *

I have no idea how but I am able to find enough stamina to carry on dashing to any direction but to escape from those heavy footsteps. If it were possible for the sounds to have colors, this stubborn, devilish stampede that rumbles behind me, making it harder for me to breathe, would be as dark as the peak of the night . . . I have probably been here for more than half an hour, running away from that "thing" living next door, that dark silhouette disappearing behind the canvas curtains . . . I try to keep quiet to keep myself hidden, but I have no other way, I have to get away from here, I have to run . . .

And I take another turn and with my lungs gasping another heavy breath, I realize the light has become brighter . . . and much lighter . . . darkness begins to draw back, it has to, I am still at the last class of school, I am not even fully grown up yet, I do not deserve any of this, I want to hug my mum, at home I crave to be . . . I have to take another large step, I must! And another, one more pace, god, please, only one more, keep that dark thing away from me, please, I . . . I . . . And with a loud sigh escaping from my weary chest, I wake up.

CHAPTER 3
HALLOWEEN

Halloween. All Hallows' Eve. October 31st arrived. It must have been the suspense for this day that caused such a terrible nightmare. One would think that as soon as I woke up, I would feel the relief of it only being a bad dream, but I was feeling that same consciousness living around me . . . again. I could constantly hear those noises coming from the house next door— the whispers, screeching and quiet strolling . . . This "only a bad dream" was carrying a strange touch of reality. Until then, I had never seen a dream so peculiar, so horrifying and so . . . *realistic*.

I loved Halloween to my core. Even more than Christmas. I believed that this was the time when the truth was the hardest to hide—I knew it sounded weird, but I considered that deep down, any person realized that the existence of mysteries was the most real and "human-ish" thing that had been created. Mysteries even were the reason of people's existence–a love for puzzling events have often been a passion for lots of human-beings . . . even for me. I was feeling a strange connection to them, as if the unknown were the sweet prey of mine, as if I were a cat stretching cozily before the crackling fireplace. I believed that mysteries gave much more meaning to life, the reason to observe and carry on living the boring routine of each new day . . . they were spice of usuality.

But now I was feeling an odd thing in my personality. A touch of fear and that nightmare turned out to be just enough for me to question my passion for mysteries. Yet, there I was, telling myself over and over again, that it was just a nightmare and the strange events were just the result of my puzzled imagination. Turning a blind eye to it was not that hard . . . After all, it was Halloween, the day of my personality flourishing, the day of my friends and me just having a good time with each other, playing "trick or treat", collecting sweets and creating unforgettable, innocent childhood memories together . . . "Okay, not quite innocent", a quick thought crossed my mind, making me chuckle.

I was always wearing a costume of the witch. Green eyes, pale skin, waist-length dark curly hair—what else to wish for!

"Only a long-style, dark dress and the trick will already be made" I said to myself and laughed for the first time in days, forgetting about that strange neighbor and my nightmare as well. But I would have to remember them in the boundary of that day and night, after the golden sun rays had gilded their way behind the surrounding hills.

* * *

The Halloween evening was more pleasing than ever before, with a touch of odd gothic beauty. It was an excellent time for the unknown to flourish. Birds were chirping harmoniously whilst the setting sun was shining in the dimly lit sky as blue as sapphire. The naughty, golden sun rays were glowing in my garden like thousands of tiny, glittering diamonds. The fir-trees, standing proudly in the boundary of the day and night, were being shaken by the light, warm breeze which was softly whispering through the shadowy trees. Air was full of the charming scent of different colored leaves which awakened many-colored dreams and on which the birds were warbling the lullaby to the setting sun.

Whilst the bright sun—as yellow as amber—was crawling across the turquoise blue sky, hiding behind the dark, emerald green fir-trees, playing peekaboo with my joyful eyes, the silvery goddess of the night was growing larger. It looked like a lonely, fluffy cloud at first, but after the darkness and the light had mixed in each other with a wild sway and the sun had disappeared behind the grassy hill, the mysterious gray moon soon formed into a perfect circle . . . It seemed as it was wearing silvery attires, as picturesque and full of glorious melancholy as autumn. I could feel an extremely pleasing feeling overtaking me which made my beating heart as lively as the Halloween mood, float up above with the shiny stars.

This magical "autumn heaven" of Earth created the atmosphere of perfection and peace, but I was also sensing something peculiar. Something was just off. It is not just a coincidence that even the best eyesight can get mistaken in a nice, pleasant twilight. Something was odd because I could feel that evil reality of the fact that, sometimes, unexpected horrible things happen after the great pleasure comes to an end . . . After all, it gets chilly quiet before the storm.

* * *

"I will catch you guys later . . . I will just . . . pop into my house for a moment" I could not believe what I was hearing out of my very own mouth, but there I was, telling this phrase to my friends—classmates and pals from the neighborhood, dressed in various costumes—scary witches, black bats, white phantoms and ghosts which were much more likely to cause sadness and misery rather than fright.

"Are you sure?" asked Andy, a little boy in the costume of an enormous pumpkin, holding a basket of colorful lollipops and other candies.

"I am," I said without any hesitation, as if I was trying to assure—not them—but my very own self. And assurance was something I definitely needed right there and then as we were standing in front of the house next door.

"Okay then, we will see you at the end of the main street, at Mrs Smith's house," a dozen hands rose in the air, waving me back, heading to the end of the street.

Then they disappeared.

Just the thought of standing about ten meters away from this house gave me chills, but I had to find out what was going on for good. That strange consciousness existing around me, as if it was watching me day and night, had already become unbearable. I had to find out what was going on . . . Love of mysteries made its job.

"It's a perfect timing," I was telling myself, assuring, and nervously grabbing the basket of sweets, "Just knock on the door and ask for a candy or two. Trick or treat!"

Every step taken towards the wooden porch of the house was making me feel more and more fragile inside. But it was already too late to stop. What was there to worry about so much after all? It was just a neighbor I hadn't seen yet. "I will just ask for a candy, that's all!"

Slowly repeating the text in my heart over and over again, I raised my slightly shaking hand to knock on the door . . .

But it was not necessary at all. The door slowly creaked open as soon as I stepped a foot on the porch.

* * *

"Hello? Is anybody there?" I asked with a trembling voice, trying to look calm and confident, "Trick or treat!"

For a minute or two I was waiting. In vain. No one seemed willing to answer me. Perhaps it was just a pressure caused by my presence on the porch, resulting in the door opening by itself. It had to be that way—I could see no one in the hall.

"Hello? Is anybody there?", asking once more, I slowly stepped into the entrance hall. The wooden floor kept creaking and those noises were quite scary, I must admit. I had been here a few times before to visit Maeve. I remembered her family had never redecorated the house, which is why the house was so creaky.

I looked around with a heartfelt attempt to find any sign of life inside, but I could see nothing on the first floor. Realizing I was not feeling so scared anymore, I decided to take a look on the second floor—the room in which I had seen a dark silhouette was upstairs, on the left, right next to the bathroom . . .

I prepared myself for the huge probability of the staircase creaking like a dying being's last breaths and slowly made my way towards the floor above. On the seventh stair—which was the last before the little smooth space from which I could see another seven stairs, poorly lit with the lights coming from the streets filled with Halloween noises—I encountered quite a strange thing.

It was a parchment. "Ahha!" I exclaimed in my head—it was the proof that someone was in this house and I definitely was not going mad. It was an old piece of thick paper, yellowed because of age, with dark stains on it. After a little hesitation, I kneeled with "one more loud last breath of a dying being" and picked it up . . . A strange poem was written on it, full of archaic words and a bizarre rhythm that was hard to catch. A poem which seemed to be terrifying yet a beautiful enchantment.

"Mysteries whisper in the peak of the night,
With the shadows dancing to the edges of sight.
Dead darkness murmurs the secret uncanny,
And marblish phantoms rise in wild sway.
These doomed dark tears mutter the unsaid
And dreams start flourishing in the wildest way . . .
Light of sun draws back in the kingdom of black,
The bittersweet darkness is calling me within!
Gazing into the mirrors of soul in reflection of mine,
I'll say: Drenched in dark ink will thy erelong be,
Letting black curtains clash upon thee!"

By this time, curiosity had conquered my inner self with the fullest meaning of the word. I looked up and continued my little adventurous journey above.

The only thing I saw upstairs before I would desperately run out of the house with a loud scream absorbing into the Halloween noises coming from the streets—with my heart bursting out from my chest and with a parchment in my hand, even forgetting that I was holding it, was the mirror—the one and only thing I caught a glimpse of when I went upstairs. The mirror which I had never seen before. The mirror that was placed right in front of the stairs across the room.

The room which showed no reflection.

CHAPTER 4
BEYOND THE MIRROR

Without slowing down, I crashed into my bedroom, dragged the curtains to fully cover the windows, walking back and forth in order to calm myself down to find any logical reason for it . . .

"What logic? How could I let myself enter into that house in the first place?! And how on earth was it possible for a mirror not to reflect?! And that strange poem . . . " I almost yelled.

The poem . . . only then I realized that the parchment was still in my hand. I was desperately holding it, as if it was the way of protection. *As if . . .*

Sitting down by the desk, I began a series of attempts to find out what the poem was about. Deep down I knew that these odd words were the key to the secret. I was feeling like a seeker, like a real mystery searcher, a witch with a chant in her hand . . .

"After all, it could be just a Halloween joke by any of my pals . . . " I laughed sarcastically at that thought.

After rereading it for the third time, I realized that there was a signature in dark black ink under the poem. Soon after that, I found out that stains on the parchment were reddish dark, with a strange origin . . . Those crimson dots did carry quite hazardous vibes . . . But what scared me to the core was not those dark spots nor the signature under them.

There was another, barely noticeable but still clear, crimson red signature under the first one.

"*DEVIL,*"it said.

* * *

Gasping loudly because of such an unpleasant discovery, I got taken aback and whilst trying to put this doomed dark pact or whatever it was back on the desk, I found myself having cut my finger on it. A few drops of blood covered the yellowish piece of paper.

Scared and confused, I instinctively put my cut finger inside my mouth, looking up.

Next thing I saw was house next door . . . My friends had just turned to another street, disappearing from my sight. It was dark and the streets were poorly lit. The house seemed larger and higher than usual, that fright I was feeling was growing larger and larger. I sensed an uncanny feeling of déjà vu overtaking me, making it hard for me to maintain balance on my very own feet . . . And then, I felt an indescribable feeling of being pushed from my back into the house.

"Oh my goodness, what is going on?!" No matter how hard I tried to scream, it did not seem that it would stop that "thing"— would stop, dragging me into that very same route I had just used – the porch, the hall, the staircase, the seventh stair . . .

The mirror . . .

I could not move my own legs as if someone or something had taken control over me. I felt shaken to the core, I was trembling from my head to toe, I was screaming internally but all in vain—that indescribable power knocked me *straight into the mirror.*

* * *

I fell down on the ground. The pain I felt, those mind blowing occurrences I just had, I had no idea how to come to my senses and hold my breath. Lying on the humid ground with a salty smell of the water, the slight tremble creeped into my body, slowly filling me up. Freeze ran in my whole shape. With a slow motion, I pulled my hair from my face, blocking my sight . . .

Right beside me, in front of the mirror with no reflections, there was a huge, dark greenish bog, with terrible smell and a queer gurgling noise . . .

And there, in front of my very own body it did stand, high and vain, picturesque and grotesque, enormous and startling, macabre and abnormally beautiful—the stone castle, dark and mysterious, with pitch black and cold towers with gothic spires and columns on it . . . odd yet absolutely magnificent. The gloomy tops of the steeples were surrounded by the silvery grayish light. The moon shone down on them, like a melancholic goddess of the night, like a crystal in the dark, magical sky. It looked like a piece of ice, frozen to the core, macabre and grotesque, like a consciousness existing around me as well as the others, laughing down on our boring everyday lives . . .

Right after I had my breath caught, beholding the unimaginable outer world surroundings, that horribly familiar feeling of being pushed from behind found its way back to me, pulling me up in the air, with my feet barely touching the dark greenish, muddy ground below, and flew me over the stone, grotesque and ancient staircase, making me head towards the heavy, large wooden door of the castle, which slowly creaked open and I felt every inch of my body floating through it, slowly changing the moment I entered inside the hall . . .

I was not a typical twenty-first century girl anymore. I found myself in the peak of the mysteries that could ever exist in the Milky Way or even beyond. I was wearing a mid-century dress of a baroness, deadly red with black stripes on it . . . I could see the most beautiful sight I had ever seen in my life—dozens of phantom-like figures dancing and strolling their way gracefully and astonishingly, with their feet barely touching the ground, wearing Venetian masks, jewelry and colorful gowns with the valuable ribbons swaying elegantly in the air, warmed by the huge fireplace in the center of the wall, in which the reddish flames of fire were reaching up to the sky and quickly disappearing into the darkness, as if the blackness kidnapped the daughter of light . . .

The hall was amazingly large, with glorious ornaments and paintings of prancing nymphs, pans and lovely child cupids on the walls and ceiling. The golden chandeliers were attached to the silvery ropes hanging down from the colorful ceiling. There was another source of light inside the room—from the gothic window of the magical castle I could see the obscure gray moon up above the sinister moor. Right in front of me, a huge organ was placed on which a graceful figure was playing *Danse Macabre*.

All of a sudden, a ghost-like silhouette, shone down by the cold rays of the moon, made his way out of the dancing crowd, slowly approaching me, with a golden mask on his mysterious face, wearing mid century, dark green suit, with a slight smile curling on the edges of his lips . . . he had barely visible reddish horns sticking up from its black, curly hair . . . slightly bowing, he drew his right, veiny arm towards me:

"Here we have another pretty one," grabbing my hand, we both darted into the dancing crowd.

Suddenly, I heard a large, wooden door slamming right behind my back . . .

And I woke up, sweating and coughing.

* * *

With a chaos in my mind, I dashed into the first thing I saw after I had woken up— the only things I could consider as the key to these horrific things . . .

Breathing heavily, I looked over it and found the most unnatural, otherworldly, spine-chilling, abhuman and peculiar thing that could ever happen . . .

Those new blood drops of mine were soiled, staining much larger area of the parchment. And to my horror, downwards, in the left corner of the page, the exact same, third signature had appeared, so clear that it was already beyond nightmarish.

"Devil."

CHAPTER 5
NOT SO DARK ANYMORE?!

It was enough. I had enough. I could not take this anymore, I had to find out once and for all what on earth was going on. For more than four months I was saying nothing to anyone about those strange happenings in order to keep myself safe from being perceived as crazy . . . But this had to stop, I had to say something to mama, to papa, to . . . anyone.

"Muuum! Mama, the neighbour next door, who is he? Or she? Why have we never seen him? How come he never steps outside the house? And what about those noises coming from the house next door? What about that . . . "

I had to stop my anxious speech when I saw horror growing into mother's eyes, enlarging more and more when I was pouring out the sentences, flowing like a mountain river. She kept looking at me with a surprised look and told me the words which reached the darkest depths of my core and which I will never ever be able to forget till this day:

"*Sweetheart, are you alright? What on earth are you talking about?! No one has lived in that house for months! Maeve and her family were the last ones to live there . . .*"

EPILOGUE

I closed my diary, still holding a pen in my sore hand, exhausted to have written more than nine pages of my *previous life*—the life I had there, in the sweet house with my family, where I was feeling safe and loved, where I grew up . . . Where I fell for the affection of mysteries which led me ... here, doomed to dance each night for eternity, locked and trapped in here because of my unforgivable curiosity.

I led myself here. Love of mysteries was my biggest passion since I remembered myself logically thinking. My destiny it that love turned out to be . . .

Did I even accidentally cut my finger on that damned old

parchment?!

I was sitting by the enormous, dark-shaped window of the gothic, magical castle from which all I could see was the sinister swamp and the mirror placed on the hill next to it.

The mirror which had no reflection.

* * *

"Mysteries whisper in the peak of the night,
With the shadows dancing to the edges of sight.
Dead darkness murmurs the secret uncanny,
And marblish phantoms rise in wild sway.
These doomed dark tears mutter the unsaid
And dreams start flourishing in the wildest way . . .

Light of sun draws back in the kingdom of black,
The bittersweet darkness is calling me within!
Gazing into the mirrors of soul in reflection of mine,
I'll say: Drenched in dark ink will thy erelong be,
Letting black curtains clash upon thee!
D."

THE CLOCK

PRIYANKA SHRESTHA

No matter how quickly the leaves seem to be changing into their fall suits, the sun always seems to slouch itself awake in the slowest of manners in those clear, first days of autumn when it's too cold for lemonade, but not cold enough yet for hot chocolate. It was on such a day, just as the sun's rays were enveloping a particular street in golden fire that a young woman opened her eyes and instinctively tightened her clammy hands around the fist of her three-year-old son.

They woke up in a foreign house, on a foreign bed, wearing a foreign and unsettlingly pitch black blanket. Her eyes were languishing under heavy bags and she found her voice hoarse and pained. Her arms where she carried her son ached most uncomfortably.

She was the kind of mother who carried a sleep monitor in her purse and had for the first year after her son's birth always woken up in the middle of the night to check if her son was still breathing. Her nightstand at home was cluttered with parenting books and Mozart CDs. She sat on the musty bed and remembered as if in a trance, "Don't waste a second of time with your children, for they will no longer be children by the time you have energy," Dr. Hoffman, from *Parenting after the 9-5*. She missed that nightstand terribly, and longed to brush against it on her way to bed, to roll over and grab a cookie from her stash of late night snacks in the second drawer.

"Good morning, Mommy!" snapped from her thoughts, the young mother shifted her attention to her little boy who had moved from beside her to nestle snugly in her lap. He looked up at her and smiled, showing a row of bright white baby teeth, sprinked freckles, dimpled cheeks, and sky-high blue eyes. All these he got from his father. His mother smiled softly. She admired the way his summer tan had started to wear off and left his skin a unique oaky golden.

150

"Morning my munchkin," she whispered.

Abruptly the woman's cell phone rang its shrill call. She picked it up hastily, glanced at the familiar number and took a deep breath. "Hello, my love."

"Morning, babe. Is he up?" The voice at the other end was deep and slightly out of breath.

"Of course," the woman.

"Keep him well for me."

"Always."

"And remember, don't leave my parents house, the neighborhood's not safe."

"Okay."

She hung up the phone and inhaled deeply, resting her head back. She scooped up her child, deciding it would be okay to spoil him this day. After all, being stuck inside her late in-laws' house didn't lend itself to much fun. Why her husband sent her and her son spend the weekend there she still could not fathom. "It'll be a fun weekend trip, you know, a change from everyday life," he insisted.

The house was old, but sturdy. It was fairly modest as most houses go: wood floorboards lined most of the interior and often found itself creeping into part of the walls, the tops of which were scattered with petrified heirlooms and antiques forever frozen in a time that had been forgotten. Most were inexpensive, the exception being an upstairs armorium and a loud grandfather clock propped against the second floor landing leading to the stairs. It was quite a beautiful looking clock, well kept and glistening as most such elegant clocks were. Upon its face—a sure sign of its expense—someone had delicately painted lovely young children frolicking through a meadow with gold gilded wings. *Children our Angels* was written neatly below. Its arms, perhaps the most peculiar attribute did in fact very much resemble human arms, though much smaller than average and possibly a bit less delicate, but other than that the clock was magnificent.

All this, the mother passed without a care. She was not into antiques and was much too busy with her son.

Downstairs an antenna radio droned lazily, its sounds creaking languidly through the dusty floorboards. "Police report the disappearance of a five-year-old girl from Westbrook county. The child was last seen on the corner of Hearthen and Streep road. Authorities ask anyone who has information to speak out." The mother spent the day making waffles and scrambled eggs, mac and cheese, and strawberries dipped in chocolate—any child's greatest dream. She and her son watched his favorite TV show, his favorite movie, sang his favorite song, and she even ran around the house with cushions on her back as the newest installment of the teenage mutant ninja turtles, falling to a dramatic, twitching, end when her son jabbed a cracked broken sword towards her.

She didn't even worry about the news reporters' voices wandering through the halls the whole day, knowing well that the radio remote would be hidden somewhere impossibly difficult to find in the house. Her in-laws had been unusually paranoid people.

Her husband called her often to check up on her. "How are things my love?"

She would always answer the same, "Fine, as always."

"Bored at all?"

"No, just spending some mother son time."

"Well enjoy it while you can. I'll try to come visit you guys tomorrow."

Her husband was a surgeon and he was often away during the day. Had they been at their usual home she would probably run some errands and been busy doing housework. She had always wished for just one day to spend to its entirety with her son. *Perhaps this is the perk of his parent's creepy old house,* she thought.

She kissed her son too many times to count, and made him laugh until they both tumbled onto the foyer rug like shapeless blobs.

The mother and son moved throughout the house like a candle illuminating the darkness. They broke the dull rhythm it had maintained since the previous inhabitants had died and caused the dust to rise up in gusts and fall in wicked, twisted ways.

Towards the end of the day the mother noticed some of the neighbors taking out their trash can for the next day.

She called her husband and asked, "Do you want me to take out the trash?"

"No, no don't worry about it, I'll do it when I get there."

"When are you coming?"

"Looks like it will be tomorrow morning, I have an amputation to do tonight."

"Alright, see you then, love you."

"Love you."

By dusk her son's energy had begun to reach the bottom of its reservoir, and he sat lazily in the master bed. She combed his hair lovingly and in the luminance of the setting sun she adored even more the bronzed glow of her son's skin.

At one moment she thought she heard the sound of a door closing downstairs, and though she strained her ears she never heard anything else. Right then her son put his head down on her lap.

"Mommy my head hearts."

She felt his forehead for any sign of a temperature, and feeling none decided that he just needed some rest. "Looks like we had a little too much fun today huh? Why don't I sing you a lullaby to sleep, you won't be hurting anymore in the morning, okay?"

"Okay, Mommy." Her son moved drowsily. "Is Daddy coming, too?"

"No darling, he's coming tomorrow morning probably."

"I think he'll come early just for me."

"Hmm, maybe, now shhh close your eyes." She sang to him in a soft voice that almost disappeared into the walls and in the process didn't even realize as she slipped off into slumber as well.

* * *

In the morning the mother woke up with a start. There was something wrong about the house. Its air hung stale and low, and the whisperings and creakings of the woods the day before ceased to a sickening silence. The mother felt her arm limp on the blanket and realized her son was not there.

She got up and felt unwell, her head spun with some invisible fog that reeked. It curled in through her nose and muddied her mind. She staggered out of bed and stumbled down the staircases coughing and dizzy. The rooms spun around her like a carousel. In her haste she passed by a carbon monoxide detector that beeped faintly. In her haste she passed by the clock on the second floor landing without looking close enough.

Outside, this day was almost the same as the day before. The grandfather clock on the wall had been changed slightly. The little arms were now golden.

LITTLE FIRES EVERYWHERE

Nicole Li

The ghosts come knocking at night, searching for a place
to go and I turn them away because these stories always

have predictable endings—tears dropping like
bombs or a room full of strangers with gaping blackholes

for mouths and teeth for eyes. No one wants to remember their
first grade birthday party or the pasta they ate before puking

in front of the whole class. I count sheep in every language
I know until I can't think of the next number,

imagine myself some alien with no past or future, a teething
thing that doesn't know much besides how to suckle.

It's easy for a while because everything's different
under the moonlight, stretched-out and strange like the skin

around old people's elbows that you have to say isn't
flaccid even though it is. Still, once you roll over they're

always hiding under the pillow in the sheets between
the springs. Careful, they'll bite fingers and toes, coax every

unwilling conversation and memory from your mind like fish
until finally, sleep drives them to the ground.

GHOSTING

ARTEMISIO ROMERO Y CARVER

I worry about your home life
must be hard at a haunted house
I wonder about your afterlife
I never see you in the sunlight
Sorry, is my dog bugging you?
Guess what they say about canines and the paranormal is true
I'll get the lights, can you close the door?
Sorry I'm so nervous
I've just never been with a ghost before

MY EMOTIONAL HISTORY WITH ZOMBIE MOVIES

JIMMY FRANCIS

Do you ever watch zombie movies? Do you ever find yourself getting irritated by the people in the zombie movies when they act like they've never seen a zombie movie before? It takes them forever to figure out the rules. Like: you have to shoot, stab or otherwise destroy the brain to kill/stop the zombies. If you shoot, stab or harm ANY other part of the body ... they just keep coming. You can decapitate a zombie and the decapitated head can still bite you and kill/turn you into a zombie. It takes them forever to figure out that there is no reasoning with the zombies, they don't care what you have to say or offer, they just want to bite, claw and eat your flesh! Not to mention that there is always someone who refuses to believe that, no matter how much they love someone, if they have been bitten by a zombie, sooner or later they WILL turn into a zombie! It takes them forever to figure out these rules. Every time. I mean c'mon already...get a clue! I can understand if it's an early zombie movie like 1968's *Night Of The Living Dead,* but if the movie takes place in present day, we're really supposed to believe the people in the movie have never seen a zombie movie, TV show, comic book/graphic novel or even HEARD of zombies??? I don't think so!

I wasn't always this jaded. Zombie movies used to REALLY scare the crap out of me. I think Denis Hopper summed up how I used to feel about zombie movies in *The Land Of The Dead* when he said "zombies man, they really freak me out!" I was about four years old the first time I saw a zombie movie. Friends of my parents we were visiting and were watching the original Night Of The Living Dead on TV and the scene where zombies are bursting through windows, doors, and walls scared me immensely. Nothing stopped them! FREAKED ME OUT MAN! Freaked me out. Several years later, I tried to watch another zombie movie. There was NO way to stop them! This movie didn't even allow people to stop zombies by destroying

157

the brain! It ended with the three survivors finding refuge from the zombies in an attic, coming across a phone number for a government agency to call in case of zombie crisis. They called it, the person on the other end of the phone took their information and location and told them help was on the way. The survivors thought they were saved, the government agency sent nuclear missiles to destroy the infested town, completely disintegrating the zombies, the town, and the human survivors as well! FREAKED ME OUT!!! Once I learned there actually was a way to stop/kill zombies, I felt MUCH better and am able to enjoy zombie movies, TV shows, books, comic books, graphic novels, video games and more.

Do you ever think to yourself what it would be like to live in a world where zombies are real? The true horror that existence would be? Society is gone, it's a daily struggle to survive. You have to try to find food and shelter, avoid radioactive and toxic waste. You have to avoid being attacked by uninfected humans who have chosen to be evil, violent, cruel, murderous and worse, not to mention the FLESH EATING ZOMBIES! Do you ever think about the living nightmare that would be? Then do you ever think: at least I wouldn't have to worry about being summoned to report for jury duty anymore?

THE AUTUMN RAG

LUCIA MARGARITA FOLLMAN

The October evening light faded like a melting candle between the trees. The wind scraped closer to the ground, stirring helpless circles of crackling amber leaves. Burying my hands deeper into my jacket pockets, I surveyed the rest of the park for him. For my younger brother, time was a matter to be generally disregarded and to be observed only for the most routine of events. The habit had stayed with him as we grew into adults.

"Reagan!" My brother Ernest cheerily greeted me from behind. We exchanged the usual pleasantries—anything else would have breached our informal pact of pacifying conversation. That's what happens, I suppose, when your only communication with someone for five years is a couple of letters asking about the wife and kids.

"It's a shame you missed Father's funeral," I remarked. "If you'd left Germany a day sooner, you could've spared me the burden of being the only child of the deceased there. The relatives targeted me as the object of pity."

He laughed a bit too amiably for my taste. "Germany was a blast. You should visit sometime whenever you're not so busy with your accounting work." He chuckled again, inhaling heartily through his cigar.

"Which brings me to why I asked you here tonight," I said quickly, not wanting to hear all of the fascinating details of his European lifestyle. "Now that Father's gone, his financial records will need to be reviewed, in conjunction with his will. You know Mother never had a mind for that sort of thing." He nodded a little more soberly, and I continued.

"So tomorrow morning I've arranged to have us meet with his executive staff for a full-scale review of his company's status. I haven't seen the will yet; Mother has it, but I can only presume the profits will be split down the middle between us." He blinked, and I decided to change the subject.

"But enough about that. Why don't we spend the evening together, catch up on the past few years? I know—you could even play those old tunes on the piano like you used to before our college days."

Ernest chuckled hesitantly, shivering in the dry wind. "I—I suppose we might as well, now that you've dragged me across the Atlantic," he added, shooting a crafty smile. "But where would you suggest we go? *You* don't have a piano."

I smiled a bit slyly as the wind picked up. "I know a place."

St. Michael's Cathedral was a short distance from the park, preceded by a twisted path strewn with scarlet leaves like magma. The trees flanking the entrance had grown considerably since our childhood; they now stretched into a vaulted, creaking tapestry of branches set against the papery yellow sky. The cathedral itself was a limestone beauty, albeit a crackling one, designed after the medieval cathedrals in France. As soon as we approached the steps, I knew he'd recognize it.

"Reagan, you bastard!" He punched my shoulder like we were teenagers, and I gave a begrudging smile. We'd been altar servers here from the time we were eight to eighteen. After the last service, we'd hide in the sacristy until the cathedral was empty, then we'd come out and Ernest would play Joplin and Clementi and Broadway tunes, both of us singing along with horrible falsetto and pretending to drink the communion wine. Anything we'd heard on the radio he could play by ear—he was amazing. He received a music scholarship that took him to Austria, then he finally settled as a pediatrician in Germany.

Talented bastard.

Ernest pushed to door open slightly, his lips tense on his cigar. "Are you certain Father Filbert isn't here?" He joked, but I could tell only partly.

"Oh, yes. He's been dead for the past five years."

Together we entered the cathedral.

"Shall we?" I gestured to the piano bench with a flourish once we were inside. We took our seats, him sitting on the right half and me sideways on the left.

Ernest spat out his cigar and began to play. "The Entertainer" rang out into the dark, cavernous nave. It was an old piano, a rare sort of upright one with a spacious interior attached behind the strings—large enough for a child to fit in, or even a lean man.

He moved on to "Easy Winner," one of our old favorites. When he reached the jingling, high-octave section, I trilled along nonsensically, exaggerating the awkward notes. Grinning, he played along with it, accenting the off-beats. The song quickly turned into an utter hysterical mess.

Some time later we pulled out the communion wine from the sacristy. The two of us drank from the goblets with relish. He continued playing jazz and ragtime, his torso bouncing as he kept adapting the tune to our nonsensical inventions. At one point I poured the remainder of his goblet down his shirt, like a sort of twisted baptismal rite. Laughing, he played with increased fervor, ending the song with a punchy discordant flourish. A bead of combined sweat and red wine trickled down his neck.

"Impressive," I remarked. "You managed to stay sober with the alcohol concentration of a dead man."

"No thanks to you," he panted, drizzling a little wine through my hair. The intoxication in his breath was unmistakable.

When he started to play one of Clementi's classical tunes, I groaned and chucked a missal at him. "Oh, God, not that one."

"Alright, alright," Ernest assented. "Okay, listen to this one," he added unnecessarily. "This is my favorite."

I immediately recognized the jovial opening notes of "Maple Leaf Rag." It was a good piece for autumn, I thought, characterized by a sharp, cool melody and nutty undertones. When he finished, I smiled politely.

"You always ended your little shows with that one." He nodded reminiscently, gazing down at the keys.

"Do you remember what you always did after playing?" I pressed on.

Ernest responded with that old characteristic grin of his,

the one that infatuated young girls and made adults suspicious. Using my shoulder as a booster, he heaved himself up to the top of the piano and reached for the latches. He paused, and I felt intensely anxious for a moment.

"Do you know something, Reagan? I—" He gave a short laugh of disbelief—"I just realized I haven't had this much fun in five years." He looked down at me with bright, youthful eyes. "I'd like to thank you for that."

I gave him a broad, self-contained smile and helped lower him inside the piano.

"I still fit!" Ernest laughed like a child. "I'll be darned...close it, Reagan, to see if I really fit all the way." As he compacted himself further down, I shut the lid and deftly latched it.

Ernest's voice was muffled beneath the dense wood, his chuckle without its usual resonance. "You didn't need to latch it, for Christ's sake. But I fit!—I fit like I was eighteen . . ." His voice trailed off, and I heard a few bumps.

"Alright, Reagan, let me out."

I didn't move.

"Reagan, open up!"

A cool silence.

I remember how he started shouting after that, how the impatience in his voice eventually gave way to angry terror. I only responded to his screams by calmly taking a seat at the piano and playing the one song I knew, the one he would play over and over . . .

Ernest made wild sounds like a madman, rattling and heaving his strength against the instrument as "Maple Leaf Rag" rang out. I played increasingly louder, trying to conceal his noise. I needed him gone, I thought seethingly. I wanted him entombed in his own passion. He had no real need of Father's profits—an accountant's salary was nowhere near a doctor's.

He screamed like a banshee, demanding to be released. I casually looked around, still playing, and noticed a few paintings on the walls, almost bright in the darkness with streaks of scarlet. There were strange sculptures, too, that I hadn't noticed before, adorning the pillars— life-size carvings of angels with colorless vigilant eyes. A bit shaken, I played the song over and over until

Ernest's rattling began to subside and his screams faded to a whimper.

One long minute of creaking passed.

Silence.

Exhaling, I stiffly shut the key lid. I gathered up my jacket and what remained of Ernest's cigarette pack, then, avoiding the sculptures' gaze, walked briskly down the aisle towards the doors. I was about to exit when I heard a creaking.

It was coming from the piano.

Cautiously, I walked back up the altar and stared at it. One of the pedals was shifting up and down. I drew in a shaky breath. I'd heard of how on chilly nights like this, strong gusts of wind could seep through old buildings and disturb the inside—

Then the music began to play.

Frozen, I stared at the instrument, not daring to lift the key lid. The "Maple Leaf Rag" played ever so softly, seeming to spiral up towards the sculptures. The angels' gaze bore into me with uncompromised finality, their faces suffused with twisted condemnation. Frantically, I swiveled back to the piano, accidentally knocking over a goblet in the process. Dark red wine splattered across the wood.

I looked up, with vague desperation, but my eyes stopped short on the wall. The scarlet painting, painted with fire and blood, depicted the agony of sinners being dragged into a chasm. They had shrunken bodies and haunting, screaming faces. As I stared into a man's open mouth, I could almost hear my brother's piercing cry, resurrected by the music. The song, the angels, the sinners, the wine. . . My head pounded and pulsed beneath the cacophony. Half-mad, I ran down the altar and was almost at the door when I slipped on something smooth in the dark. My head bluntly hit the floor, and, just before I lost consciousness, I felt a gust of cool autumn wind from beneath the door.

I woke up in the hospital, a janitor having found me early in the morning. The only words of real significance I caught in my daze were 'intoxication' and 'concussed'. When I returned home that afternoon, I found a letter wedged in the mail slot. I opened it and read the contents—first with curiosity, then horror.

Dear Ernest,

I thought you might be staying with your brother, considering you never responded to my previous letters— presumably out of shame.

I know your circumstances have been difficult for the past few years, jumping from job to job in Germany and Melinda eventually leaving you before you could go bankrupt. Overall, I think it was best that the rest of the family knew nothing more than that you were a successful pediatrician.

But things have changed now, and with the loss of your father comes a new opportunity for you. Before he died, we agreed the business was to be split between you and Reagan. This was mostly done for your benefit—while your brother makes a steady enough income, we wanted to keep you from living off the streets—as I'd heard you'd been doing in the past month.

It's never too late to start over, to begin a new life for yourself. I wish you all the best.

Love,

Mother

THE PROPHETESS

GRACE PENG

It seemed too quiet to be real. After all, New York City is a city dubbed one that 'never sleeps.' But it was dead silent during the blue hour of twilight, no curses spewing out of angry taxi drivers, no beeping phones, no police sirens, no nothing.

Thunder rumbled in the distance and from the Earth issued a raven-haired woman. Her eyes were amber yellow, slit-pupiled, cat-like if you will. She wore no shoes, but shimmering onyx spirals swirled around her ankles and wrists, a circlet of silver thorns perched on her charcoal hair. Despite the fact that it was in the middle of the summer, July 31st to be exact, this woman bore no hint of a tan on her ivory skin, possibly save for beige freckles sprinkled around her forearms. A flowing Greek chiton covered her body, brushing her calves, a rich jet color resembling her hair. The stars above her seemed to glow more brightly than normal.

With a look of displeasure thrown across the woman's arrogant features, she let a soft hiss of laughter and her right hand flew upwards, palm up, fingers spread. The sky dimmed, only the crescent moon a silvery light in the darkness.

"You can do better than that, Artemis," she whispered almost chidingly.

As quick as a flash, the woman whipped out a gold dagger seemingly out of nowhere. She cut a deep wound into both of her hands. Golden ichor, blood of the gods, dripped steadily in a slow trickle onto the ground, turning scarlet as soon as it touched the dirt and in all directions through the fertile grass, stopping at a cream circle that suddenly gleamed, Ancient Greek symbols floating around the blood, surrounding the lady.

She closed her eyes, ink strokes of her hair brushing her angular cheeks as a faint bronze glow emitted from her body as the air around her thrummed with energy and power. She flung her hands up, her arms straight, blood lips murmuring words of a long-forgotten tongue, a Summoning Spell.

"*Alligarent crinibus!*" She shouted clearly, the Latin word for enchantment echoing throughout the forest, slipping around her to form a rugged plain, an abnormal sight.

The six children came at once. Although, their eyes were wide open, they were not registering anything. The six were all dressed in nightclothes, all at six years of age. Faint auras appeared from the children, ranging from a luminescent snow to a deep violet.

"I am Persephone, children, as you may one day may know me as, or the Seer of the gods. In six years' time, you shall meet." This was a statement.

Obediently, the children one by one cut both hands and linked them, blood touching the ground and fizzing, forming a small circle as Persephone floated several feet off the ground above them.

"The blood of the heavens shall have risen,
thrice from bone,
once from blood,
twice from tears,
the half-god six shall ally against fears.

These mortals shall answer the call,
once before the world shall fall;
to rebirth or ashes they shall choose,
to assist or refuse,
as the Earth Mother has let them loose.

Bind the souls to one another,
each fate entwined with all the others,
for they are too weak to work alone.

One of intelligence,
one of the dead man's spirit,
one of ferocity,
one of prophesying,

one of magic,
one of words,
my blood binds to theirs,
wielding my secrets within their hands,
for darkness awaits in unclaimed lands." Persephone chanted.

You'd think that after all that chanting, someone would be breathing hard, or collapse if you were floating like Persephone was, but not the goddess of the underworld. A slightly musical hum filled the air as she decided the roles of the Mortal Six based on their talents and personalities. All excess blood was siphoned off the ground and the children were sent back to all corners of the world, but the damage had been done—the Curse of Ages entering their veins. Here they stumbled into their rooms until they had fallen asleep, safe and sound, not even noticing the final weight on their shoulders. One that wreaked havoc for centuries on their ancestors. The Curse of Ages was the only one Persephone had ever predicted and cursed Guardians of the Realms with. The Mortal Six this time would decide whether the people of Earth would survive the Apocalypse or fail during the Apocalypse.

THE DECEIT OF MYTHOLOGY

JENNIFER MARTOCCI

As Andrew pushed open the heavy wooden door of the Greek Mythology classroom, a blast of chill air from the room made him shudder. He froze for a second as he took in the features of the dimly lit room. The dirt-covered cinder block walls were accented with lit torches, but that wasn't what grabbed his attention. It was the strange dust-covered creature shaped statues that were scattered around the room. Thinking about it, he suspected they were creatures from Greek mythology, which only made him feel a little bit better.

He closed the stubborn door behind him. It instantly felt it hard to breathe in the musty air. Curious about this new classroom's decorations, he studied the statue closest to the door, which was of a strange creature that looked like a goat, lion, and snake rolled into one. Andrew turned away from the statue but instantly turned back to it as he saw movement. He let out a breath as he realized there was only a mirror behind the statue, and he just saw himself moving. He shook his head and reminded himself that there was nothing to be scared of here. But help as he may, he was still paranoid. He looked back into the mirror and saw a figure standing behind him. All thoughts of calmness disappeared, as he quickly revolved to face the figure. The figure was about six feet tall, towering over the relatively short Andrew. He took note of its stillness and stone-like appearance, deducing that the figure was a statue. He took in the features of the statue of Medusa, the creature from Greek mythology who had snakes for hair and could turn people to stone by staring at them. He noticed her short green dress, and most attention-grabbing, the brown snakes coming out of her head. "I'm an idiot, aren't I?" Andrew muttered loudly, annoyance with himself present in his voice after he realized that he was scared of a statue.

He glanced around the room, wondering who heard him talking to himself. Then, he finally realized that there was no one else in the room. He had been too busy concerned about the strangeness of the room that he hadn't been taking notice who else was in there. There wasn't even a teacher anywhere in sight. Had he come to the wrong classroom? He hurried out of the classroom, glad that the door came unstuck quickly. He checked the room number but determined that it was the right classroom, 132. He still had a few minutes before class actually began, so he hurried down the hallways of the school, trying to find his good friend, Jake, who would help him sort this out.

"Andrew!" a voice behind him shouted.

Andrew jumped around to face Jake, his heart pounding in his chest. "Wow, dude, you're jumpy today," Jake remarked. "Aren't you supposed to be at the Greek Mythology classroom?"

"I went there and there was no one there," Andrew started. "There were all these freaky statues, and—"

"Woah, dude, chill out, we can head over to the classroom together and figure it out, okay?"

"Alright, just don't scare me like that again."

Andrew led Jake down the hallways to room number 130, before stopping. "Is this it?" Jake asked.

"No, it's number 132," Andrew answered.

"That ain't possible, it ends at 130."

"It was right here."

"Are ya sure you weren't dreaming it up?"

"I'm positive,"

"Did ya get enough sleep last night, man?"

"Yes, the room was here," Andrew said stubbornly, raising his voice a notch. "I'm certain."

"Hush, dude," Jake said, gesturing to a nearby group of giggling girls. "You're making us looking stupid in front of these ladies," he said, giving them a smile.

The three girls giggled in response.

"Sorry," Andrew muttered quietly, distracted as he scanned the group.

He recognized two of the girls from previous years of school. He didn't recognize the tallest girl, but he definitely remembered her from something. She was wearing a short green dress that he was surprised she was able to sneak past the dress code monitors.

On top of her dress, she was wearing a black hoodie, with the hood pulled up over her head, covering her hair which seemed to be brown. The strange part of her outfit was the sunglasses that she was wearing indoors.

"Dude, stop staring at them and let's go before we make ourselves look even worse," Jake said quietly to Andrew, leading him down the hallway, past the group of girls.

"Do you know who the tall girl is?" Andrew asked Jake.

"I met her but don't remember her name. I think it started with a 'm'. Why? Do you think she's cute? She honestly gives me a creepy vibe."

Andrew turned around to the group and looked back at the tallest girl again. 'M, m, m' raced through his head. Who was this girl? Then it hit him.

She looked back at him as he tried to back away. She took off her sunglasses in one swift motion and stared him in the eyes.

He took in every detail of her eyes: the soft hazel brown color with specks of green flurried throughout them. Her small dull black pupils. The exaggerated red veins in the whites of her eyes. Her unblinking gaze.

THE THING ABOUT
PERFECTION

MICHELLE MA

She was sure she hadn't walked this path before, and yet—that same gnarled, twisted tree root protruded from the dirt. The dark, diseased oak tree with its flaky, peeling bark. Even the wind seemed to sing the same wailing tune. She was going in circles. Her digital watch flashed 11:47. It would be dark soon. It would be too late, soon.

What seemed hauntingly beautiful mere minutes ago had taken a turn for the grotesque. She was growing desperate, breaking into a run, breathing harsh and piercing in the stillness of the air. Tonight—it needed to be tonight.

Branches seemed to reach towards her. One lashed out at her face, dragging talons across her skin and breaking it open in a sudden sting.

The toe of her black sneakers caught on something—rock, root, she would never find out—and the ground reared up to meet her.

#

Consciousness returned in a groggy daze with a dash of pain splicing her cheek.

She groaned. Pushed up with her right arm into a sitting position on the cold, rotten-leaf ground. The autumn musk was particularly heavy down here, cloying in her nose. She rubbed her eyes, feeling the grit of dirt on her face, and blinked up into the sky.

There was a house. It looked like something out of a postcard, some cozy cottage home tiled with burgundy reds and woolly grays. Silver chimes hung from the porch, and a tinkling melody filled the air; dark and sweet simultaneously.

She stood up on shaky legs. Her steps were coltish like a newborn baby deer.

Old wooden stairs creaked beneath her shoes. The door was stained with chipping lacquer. The *Welcome* mat was faded and gray.

She knocked.

Ten seconds. Silence save for the rustling of the leaves. Once more: the door clicked, then slowly swung open.

A woman stood by the doorway. She was dressed in a red-and-white checkered apron and a nightgown. Her hair fell down in thick, gleaming curls. Her eyes were completely black.

She gasped and blinked and they were gone. In their place, bright blue irises surrounded by clear white sclera peered at her inquisitively.

The woman smiled. "What's wrong, dear?"

"I—I thought—" She stammered, shook her head. Raised her hand to rub at her eyes. "Nothing. Nevermind."

"Well, aren't you a sight for sore eyes," the woman said. "Come on in, love. I'll fix you up right as rain."

"No, that's okay," she protested. "I just need some directions, that's all."

The woman tilted her head. "Oh, but you look simply *exhausted.*"

She *was* exhausted, now that she mentioned it. Her eyes drooped. Her shoulders slumped. A yawn tugged at the corners of her mouth.

"Come on in," the woman repeated. "Just for a few minutes. Get some rest before you leave, hm?"

She opened her mouth to protest again when her thoughts suddenly halted, flinched, swirled into a blur of dazed confusion. From the haze, an image floated into her head: a big, soft bed, swaddled by blankets. She really was so very tired.

The woman opened the door fully and stepped aside to give her a full view of the entrance hall, where a soft orange glow seemed to emanate.

Words formed without her command. "Okay," she mumbled. "Just a few minutes."

The woman broke into a huge smile. "The guest room's just upstairs, I'll lead you there."

A heady scent surrounded her the instant she entered the

house; crisp apples and cinnamon cider. She looked around and saw dozens of flickering candles mounted on the wall. Decor lined the tables with mini acorns and cones. The walls were inscribed with a swirling pattern that seemed to glow golden in the candlelight, pulsing with every breath she drew.

"This is . . ." She struggled for words. "This is—" (Beautiful. Astonishing. Everything she had dreamt and more.)

The light curled inside her, warming her from the inside out. In a daze, she was lead up the stairs, down the hall, through a tall door.

The guest room came in the form of a large room painted periwinkle, curtains drawn, leaving the space in a soft, damp darkness. Aided by a gentle push, she was guided to the bed— just as big and soft as she had imagined. She sunk into the mattress, bliss surging a sleepy smile on her face.

"Thanks," she remembered her manners enough to murmur.

"You're very welcome, dear," a responding whisper came. She felt a hand brush through her hair, pushing her bangs from her forehead; there came with it a soft singing voice, something oddly familiar, remembrance flitting away when she drew close like a nervous butterfly. She was asleep before she could pin it down.

#

She roused to a warm palm against her cheek and a careful whisper in her ear. "Wake up, dear."

She opened her eyes to the woman again, eyes the bluest of blue. Her hair smelled like a pine tree. "I made breakfast," she said softly.

She looked at her, then sat up and looked around at a pale, baby-blue bedroom. Sunshine streamed through the curtains. Birds sang.

A jolt of sunken confusion crossed her. "This isn't . . ."

"Don't worry," the woman soothed, the hand on her cheek coming up to smooth her hair. "It's alright, love. Everything is going to be just fine, just you see." Swiftly, she smiled. "Now, come on down. I made breakfast."

173

She blinked. A sudden cloud had overtaken her thoughts and she shook her head, hoping to clear it. What had she— something about time—

She blinked again. She was sitting at a huge wooden table that shined amber in the light. A plate sat in front of her, towered to the brim with the most perfect pancakes she had ever seen, stacked golden and fluffy and dripping with syrup.

A fork and knife lay by the side. She picked them up and cut into the stack; dark shiny chocolate oozed out. She took a forkful into her mouth and her eyes fluttered shut. Sticky syrup and sauce ran down her chin.

"I've always wanted to try these," she blurted through a muffled mouth, too eager to wait.

The woman's eyes were twinkling with joy. "I'm glad you like them."

She was halfway through her plate before she realized the woman wasn't eating. She stopped chewing (with reluctance) and looked at her. "You're not having any?"

The woman shook her head and smiled again. "I'm alright, love."

The smell of the pancakes wafted towards her again. All of a sudden, she was ravenous. Forgetting her concerns, she bent down over her plate and dug in.

When she finished, the woman took her plate over to the sink.

"Tell me, love," the woman called out, a crisp lemony scent drifting from the kitchen as she scrubbed. "How are you feeling?"

She chewed, swallowed, her last bite. "Happy," she answered quickly.

The woman turned off the tap. When she turned towards her, she was beaming. "Is that so?"

She nodded. "Happier than I've ever been."

The woman tittered. For an instant, she seemed to almost flicker. "That's phenomenal, dear. What do you say—how are you feeling about squash soup for lunch?"

The woman dried her hands and stood in front of the sink. It was a deep, square sink with a removable head. (A sudden, piercing flash of thought. The sink she had at home was small, round, and the tap too close to the far end so that the back of her hands grazed up against it every time she washed them.)

"That's . . . That's perfect." All of a sudden, her throat felt tight and sandpaper-dry.

The woman seemed too taken to notice. She clapped her hands together and smiled that brilliant smile yet again. "Perfect."

She smiled back, looking into eyes too blue to be true. Her gaze shifted behind to the walls of the kitchen, where the scribbles of light seemed to have gone brighter, almost blinding, flashing with every beat of her heart. She had run out of time.

A tremor snaked down her spine. Suddenly, she was cold.

"Funny thing about perfection," she said. "There's always a catch."

She pried her way through the fuzzy veil of soft, buzzing comfort that had coated her mind, reaching for the memorized words that seemed eons away and yanking it close. A sharp pain filled her in the form of a blazing headache. She ignored it, and began to recite in a steady voice well-practised, well-used Latin.

The woman's eyes rolled back in her head as she began to wail.

No. The word resonated through the house. The inscriptions flashed red and seemed to slither, lashing out violently. Candle flame leaped and licked the ceilings, casting wildly flickering shadows that writhed on the walls. Through all of this, she only spoke. She could not hear her words.

The woman sunk to her knees. Thick black smoke seeped from her pores.

No, no, please.

She spoke her last phrase. It emitted one final, mourning shriek, thrashing violently, before crumpling smaller, smaller so. It could not speak, but its grief rang clear as a bell through the house. Smoke poured out, thicker and thicker then, so heavy she could not see it; and with the plumes, she felt its pain. Confusion riddled with anger, hurt, betrayal, and beneath it, a loneliness so desperate and a bitterness so black she staggered under its weight.

She coughed. It dug itself into her throat, clawing its way through her chest, blinding, suffocating—

Her face was pressed harshly into the forest floor. Rotten leaves filled her mouth.

She choked and turned her face to the side. Her breaths came in wheezes as she clutched her stomach. Curling up, she began to shake, spitting up stems and dirt.

When she finally stood up, tremors ran uncontrollably down her legs and her spine. Her face was inexplicably wet, trailing warm and salty down her cheeks. Tingles crawled along her skull like hundreds of ants. A side effect—she had read all about them. (She had read all about *it*.)

She brushed dirt off her shirt and surveyed her surroundings. Above, the moon glinted a skinny silver crescent, barely seen. Pale, streaky clouds rolled through an ink-black sky. The trees made their hasty retreat, branches carefully tucked in, keeping their distance this time.

She recognized this path. All she needed was to follow it along, and she would reach the main road.

Her digital watch blinked 11:51. Where the branch had gotten her, her cheek stung with a fresh-cut pain. She touched it carefully, and then wiped her face on her sleeve.

The children should be waking, soon. The ones it took before her.

It never wished to hurt them. She recalled the desolate, boundless loneliness she had felt in those black plumes of smoke. It just wanted company. The children must've been ecstatic, too. Blissed-out, living their lives of ecstasy in its own little world, none the wiser of their true condition here (*dead, listless eyes; pulse so faint it was barely there*). Whatever they wanted. To them (*to it*), it was perfect.

It had tried so hard for her. Her mother still struck an endless pain in her heart, resonating without rest, as sharp and deadly as the day she had died. It had mimicked her appearance perfectly, not a hair out of place.

But her mother had made her plain porridge for breakfast every morning. Her mother kept her up all night with hours of overtime work in their tiny single home, lighted by one flickering candle. Her mother had a shitty sink.

The wind picked up, slowly. It ruffled her hair and blew her bangs from her face, and whistled in her ears a dark, sweet melody.

Funny thing about perfection, she thought, and made her way out of the forest.

THE INSOMNIAC

MADDIE BOTTI

In a little green house on Maple Street, there is a girl with long curls and small lips and many worries. She sits on her bed, a book resting in between her elbow and her upper thigh, staring intently at the page in front of her. The words aren't cooperating; they shift on and off the page, blurring and twisting into indecipherable blots of ink. The clock on the chipping mahogany nightstand tells her that it's well past 2 a.m., but it is so impossibly silent that it seems time shouldn't be moving at all. The quiet is absolute and stifling. There is too much thinking to be done in the quiet, and if she thinks too much, her head will run wild with untamed thoughts.

She tosses the book to the floor where it strikes two mugs, which knock against each other and threaten to spill syrupy brown on the floorboards. She should clean, but god, she is tired. At this hour of the morning, it's a special type of fatigue that takes over her. Eye-itching, bone-aching weariness that can only be cured by the blissful unconsciousness of sleep.

She sprawls out across her bed, unable to summon enough energy to pull the blanket around her. Anxieties waltz through her head, twirling together and thrusting apart: her grandmother's colorless face, her father's failure to return home almost every night, the end of her life, the end of the world (would the two collide?), that embarrassing thing she uttered last week, her mother's absence from her existence, the point of her existence, et cetera.

Only at these hours does the heart really crack open and spill its contents throughout her body in a sticky, tangible mess. The demons inside her pick the locks of their cells and roam free.

She tosses and turns, twisting white sheets around her torso.

"Jesus," she murmurs aloud, though she does not believe that Jesus can help her.

"Just one night. Just let me rest for one night."

"You want to sleep?"

Her body jerks when she hears the voice from somewhere in front of her, heart nearly pouncing out of her chest. In a flash, she is certain that she'll die, which moments ago might not have seemed like such an awful thing, but now true terror shoots through her.

A vaguely translucent figure is squatted in the corner of her room between the cluttered dresser and the heaping clothing hamper. Long, oily hair sticks to its pale scalp, and a crooked nose juts out of its face. Rags adorn what she can see of its body; silver saucer eyes peer out of a disproportionately small head, shiny and huge. It looks almost like a woman, but something is off. Not the lack of opacity, but something deeper.

The girl tries to form words, but her mind races so fast that none will materialize. She has never believed in ghosts or devils or anything of the sort. Defying all logic, the Thing scuttles toward her on short limbs like a grotesque chameleon. She shrinks back into the rough pillow.

"Don't hurt me," she gasps. Her mouth has gone dry, but her eyes fill with tears. The Thing stops in the middle of the room, which seems to have gotten smaller.

"I do not intend to hurt you," it rasps, which is no comfort. She presses her shoulder blades against the headboard, distancing herself as much as possible. "I want to help you sleep."

The situation is almost laughable.

"I must be crazy," she says, and a horrified little laugh escapes her. "Oh, why. Why, why why." She stuffs her head into the pillow, but her face is numb. People will come and collect her now, put her in some hospital. The thought itself is enough to make her want to scream.

"You are not crazy," the Thing says, and it takes a step closer. It scrapes across the floor; the sound sends shivers down her spine. "I'm just as real as you are. I can help you sleep." Its voice is like fingernails dragged across wood.

"How real am I?" the girl responds, lifting her head and meeting its large eyes. She thinks of quarters. "If you're just as real as me?"

"It matters not. Do you want to rest?"

She considers for a moment, fumbling through a tangle of thoughts. What's the worst that could happen? She hasn't slept properly in years. Her mind is messy and unmotivated. Maybe succumbing to this—whatever it is—could help her.

"Yes," she says, but her knuckles are as white as the pillowcase she clutches.

The Thing makes its way closer to her, and she wants to plug her ears from that vile sound of invisible claws scratching the floorboards.

"Then you must do something for me."

It sits—or at least, it takes on the position of what would be sitting if it were human, its body sluggish and gelatin-like on top of spindly legs—and begins to speak:

"I was once a girl like you. A beautiful, young girl with dreams and loves and struggles. It was the best time of my existence, but I didn't know it until it was gone. I want it back. I have already collected the dreams and the love and everything good. I only need the bad. And you can give it to me."

The girl relaxes her grip on the pillow, confused. "You want the bad things in my life?"

What an exchange: her hardships for rest!

The Thing nods eagerly, its thin neck bobbing the head up and down in a way that nearly makes her gag, but she doesn't avert her gaze.

"Yes! Every bad emotion, every sadness you have ever felt, I want it. Then, I will have everything I need!"

The girl sits up fully, limbs shaking, but she does not let that deter her from resting her bare feet down on the cool floor. Her mind scrambles with the possibilities. She would not have to remember her grandmother's funeral, or smell the intoxication of her father, or wallow in her lack of a mother, or tremble with existential dread, or wince at the little bits of pain that add up to something bigger, something sharper, to stab her as she lies awake. What has she to lose?

"Is it really possible?" she asks, but she already believes that it is. She can feel the verity of the promise, even though her stomach churns at the inconceivable sight in the middle of her bedroom.

"Of course it is. In this world, anything is possible, though it is rare that anybody ever acknowledges it."

"What do I have to do?" There is no trace of weariness in her now; the blood whirling in her ears gives her a rush like nothing she has ever experienced.

"Will it, and it will be done."

She eyes the Thing one last time before allowing her lids close and darkness envelop her vision. Each bad memory forces itself to the front of her mind until she feels she may implode . . .

But then they're gone. The shock of it forces her eyes open. Between her and the Thing is a great, twisted ball of mass convulsing in the air before her. If she squints, she can see the rough outline of a man lifting a bottle to his lips, which morphs quickly into a woman in a casket, the sneering face of a peer, the expression of disappointment plastered on a face that she imagines her mother's to look like, the infinitesimal globe of the earth erupting into flames. Tears rush down her face at the sight, which immediately leap off of her cheeks and join the hideous assemblage.

The Thing stands to its fullest ability and reaches out a gnarled, yellow hand while opening its jaw. Its mouth gapes for a few seconds, revealing thousands of tiny sharp teeth against a blood-red backdrop, dripping with saliva. The girl shuts her eyes again, repulsed, and a noise like a vacuum fills the air around her. This is the last thing she remembers.

When she wakes, she doesn't immediately recognize her surroundings. She is staring up at a pristine ceiling. Her face is fresh as blossomed roses; her eyes are lovely and bright. Smiling, she turns her head to the side and sees her room, sparkling clean. There is no overflowing hamper, no books littering the floor, no coffee mugs dotting available surfaces haphazardly. Everything is where it is supposed to be. She feels wonderfully tranquil, remnants of light laughter stored up inside her, waiting to be set free into the air. She inhales and smells cinnamon, and her smile grows wider.

She bounces around her new room, running fingertips over the organized and alphabetized bookshelf, dancing on tip-toe where clothing and junk used to bestrew the floor, admiring her collection of dolls, their pretty heads upright and smiling. A photograph on the wall that once contained her father's unsmiling face and a delirious note from her grandmother written days before she passed had disappeared, replaced with a picture of a clean, smiling man whom she could barely recognize (though this did not trouble her) and a neat, sweet card. She touches them, basking in the realness of the objects.

She turns and is met with the sight of a woman beaming at her though a frame directly across from the portrait of her grinning father. The woman shares her curls and eyes. She knows that the woman is proud of her, and this knowledge spreads throughout her body like a wine stain, hearty and warm.

Her attention turns back toward the bed, so pleasant and inviting that she crawls into it.

"This is wonderful," she says to nobody, listening to birds twitter outside her window.

She giggles to herself at the absurdity of it all. She could just lie here forever, and forever, and forever . . .

Her eyelids fall shut again.

The second time, it is not so nice. She blinks and rolls over onto her side, startled by a sudden emptiness in her stomach. She lies still for what feels like a hundred years until she forces herself up, unable to stand the feeling of her too-soft arms against the too-clean sheets any longer. Her parent's faces taunt her from the walls as she pads across the floor, struck with sudden curiosity, to where her mirror stands. There are no more playful lipstick stains or the shadows of fingerprints adorning it.

What she sees fills her with something familiar and unknown all at once. Something that she shouldn't feel. Something that is supposed to be gone.

Before her is a strange being. Its skin is glowing but not in an attractive way; an alarming white hue encases it. Its cheeks are too pink, its eyes too blue, its hair too glossy and long. This is not her.

She reaches out a fingertip to touch the mirror and whispers, "What are you?", not expecting an answer. The Thing stares back, its own index finger pressed to hers.

"Isn't this what you wanted?" a voice says from behind it, and in the mirror's reflection there is a woman—the girl that it once was.

She doesn't look quite the same. Some of the facial and bodily features are different, but she undoubtedly carries an unidentifiable piece of what before belonged to the Thing that it is now. There are dark circles under her eyes, a smattering of freckles across her face, and an expression that knows what the Thing once knew but can no longer summon.

"Who are you?" it asks.

"I am what you gave to me," the woman replies. "I have dreams and loves and struggles. That is what it means to be human."

THE CANDLEWICK MAN

NOAH OH

"Tatatatatata ta ta tat." My dad was drumming the car dashboard nervously. He did not want to admit it, but we were completely and entirely lost. I stared out of the window. I was starting to get car sick.

"I can't believe we are missing trick-or-treating for this!" my brother Daniel mumbled sleepily.

"Oh, shut it, Danny," my sister Violet replied, "Dad would have taken all of our candy away anyways." Danny snored in response. Daniel Curtis Drummings could have easily won a medal for being able to sleep whenever he wants to. He managed to sleep through hurricanes, chainsaw noises, and even Violet's 13th birthday party. However, the feat that really takes the cake is when he managed to fall asleep after what happened the last time we went camping at Purplewood Lakes.

****

My mind went back six years. I was only nine, Violet was seven, Danny was five, and my youngest sister Monica wasn't even born yet. Danny and I were romping around in the crisp golden leaves, laughing and tackling each other. Danny is younger than me, but I'm pretty sure that he is stronger. I had him in a half-nelson when the most peculiar feeling gripped us. We exchanged glances, then slowly pressed forward, away from camp, being very careful not to make noise. We came across a small clearing. There was a man tied up and whimpering on the floor, he saw us and whimpered some more. Another figure entered the scene. He was tall but very thin, built like a candlewick. Even his hair was patchy and burnt looking. He was holding a large meat cleaver and ambled over to the poor whimpering man. The poor fellow chanced a pleading look to me and Danny, and Danny squeezed my hand so damn hard. My hands went numb. A twig snapped; my face went even number. The Candlewick Man turned around slowly. I saw his grotesque face and it took all my effort to keep from fainting. Danny screamed, I snapped out of it and we both bolted towards camp. The man had had pins holding his skin to his face. His pupil-less eyes bulged out. Wherever he stepped he brought with him the stench of rotting flesh as well as a group of very persistent flies. The worst part was that the skin covering his face was someone else's! It hung loose in certain places, and in others, it was a bit too tight. I will never know if he chased after me or not, because I never looked back. I ran as fast as I could, dodging trees and rocks, ignoring my tired legs and frantic lungs. I was never a great athlete, tall, lanky, and a bad runner in general. However, that day not even Danny, the star-soccer player, could keep up with me. My dad was making hot dogs when we got back. He took one look at our faces and laughed.

"Let me guess, you guys saw a man with no pupils, and pins on his face," my dad said grinning, "Violet says she saw the same thing. Look, I'm all for a good prank, but you can't fool your Daddy O'. I never fall for that kind of stuff." I was in a state of disbelief. He didn't believe Danny, me, or Violet.

****

"Yes!" My dad shouted triumphantly, "My phone finally picked up a signal! Now Google Maps can lead us the rest of the way!" I snapped back to reality.

"So, you were lost!" I said with a chuckle.

"No, Daddy O' doesn't get lost. I was just in dire need of Google Maps," he snapped back. I laughed and then turned to look out of the window, I saw the familiar thin trees of Purplewood Lakes.

"In fifteen-hundred feet, your destination is on the left." The disembodied voice from my dad's Google Maps said. I hopped out of the car to stretch my legs. Then we trekked down to our

185

camping sight and unpacked. My mom unpacked our suitcases, while Dad and I set up the tents. Violet and Danny went to climb some trees.

"Stuffy, Stuffy, Stuffy, where's Stuffy?" Monica peppered mom with questions about the long, stuffed snake that Monica couldn't sleep without.

"Hold on, I need to unpack these other things first. I'll get you Stuffy in a bit," my mom answered.

"Here, I'll unpack the rest of the tents, you go play with Danny and Violet," my dad said. I turned around. "Hey, if you see our pin-faced friend, tell him I say hi." My dad said with a laugh. I went to go see what my siblings were doing. They were building a giant leaf pile. I joined in, but I couldn't stop thinking about the Candlewick Man.

"Hey! Crackerjack!" I turned around to see that Crackerjack, our dog, had urinated right into our leaf-pile. When we first got Crackerjack, we were divided between the names Cracker and Jack, so we went with a compromise.

"I don't know about you, Violet, but I don't care about dog pee. I'm jumping in. Cowabunga!" Danny yelled as he jumped into the pee-covered leaf-pile.

"Ewww Danny, that's gross!" Violet yelled.

"Come on, Violet, it's not as gross as 'Daddy O's' hot dogs." I replied with a laugh.

"That's true," Violet answered.

"It's also not as gross as the Candlewick Man." Danny replied. The comment turned into a heated discussion. My dad joined in.

"It's hot dogs for dinner!" He exclaimed to lighten the mood. We all groaned. Crackerjack's ears went down.

"Not dogs for lunch! Hot dogs, silly!" Danny told Crackerjack. Crackerjack's ears stayed down. Just the stench of my dad's hot dogs was enough to scare away all animals in a mile radius. At least the dog didn't have to eat them.

As if she was reading my mind, my mom joked, "Crackerjack is so lucky! He doesn't have to eat your hot dogs!"

My dad just rolled his eyes and went to go start a fire. We all sat around the now blazing fire and ate our hot dogs. I would describe them to you, but I wouldn't do that to anyone, except maybe the Candlewick Man. I closed my eyes, pinched my nose, and pushed the volatile, sorry excuse for a hot dog into my mouth and pretended that it was ice cream. My siblings followed suit. Dad's hot dogs are the only food that Crackerjack doesn't beg for because she hates them just as much as we do.

"I'm cooking for the rest of this trip!" My mom exclaimed joyfully. We all cheered.

"Alright kids, go frolic in the woods or whatever kids do these days." My dad said pretending to be hurt by our affront on his cooking ability.

"Honey it's 10:00, they should be getting some sleep," my mom replied. With that, we ambled over to our tents and, as "Daddy O'" likes to say it, "we hit the sack." However, long after the last smoldering embers of our fire were in the wind, and long after the soccer and sleep champion Danny fell asleep, I was still tossing and turning in bed. Every slight movement, noise, vibration, in my mind was the Candlewick Man. The Candlewick Man kept my eyes wide open, and my body trembling and covered in sweat. The wind in the trees was the Candlewick Man waiting, my dad moving in his tent—it was the Candlewick Man, shifting into position, every noise from a neighboring campsite was the Candlewick Man, pouncing. At last, after hours of torture and fear, sleep took the reins, and I was finally calm again.

I woke up to the crisp smell of autumn and the crackling sound of my mom cooking bacon. I got up on my knees and left the tent. I stretched as a brisk autumn wind swept through the trees, leaving red-gold leaves in its wake. I yawned and turned around to see my siblings playing what I think started as catch. However, at that moment it was really just Danny and Violet pegging each other as hard as they could with a rubber ball. My dad came to us asking if we had seen Monica. Usually she was up by now, but we all assumed that she was just pulling a prank on us. Still though, we searched for her, and I couldn't shake the uneasy feeling that I was getting.

"Hahaha, Mon, very funny!" I called, "Now come back, Stuffy misses you."

The only response was the wind rustling the trees. I was starting to get a little worried. Those words always got Monica to come back. Maybe I had said it wrong? I had expected her to pop out from behind a tree or something, but she didn't. I went over to her tent to make sure that she wasn't just hiding under her sleeping bag or something. I didn't find my little sister, but I did find something else.

I screamed. The rest of my family rushed over to see what happened.

"What's wrong, Tucker?" my dad asked worriedly.

I pointed. On the floor were Stuffy, two pins, and a pool of blood. That and the look on my face were all they needed to see to figure out what had happened.

"The Candlewick Man," I whispered to myself.

A Stain in the River

Sofia Pham

Moss coated the trees like thickly layered paint, wildflowers blooming sporadically nearby. The deep gurgles of the stream bellowed a slow symphony in the background.

Brown eyes shifted from the scene to a blank canvas stretched taut over wooden stakes, the sharp wrinkles pulling themselves tight against bone. Her hands, aged but steady, smeared a bead of blue onto the board, breaking the seemingly endless horizon of pure white.

A sky was born in a different world.

Where the stones laid buried in hunks of stiff mud and animal muck, she shuffled dark brown tones with a bristling brush, moving quickly while the paint was still wet. Dark hues, navy for the rising earth, breaths of white against the blue stretch of sky above her.

And those green, hulking trees, giants stumbling around the tiny creatures below them, blocking out the sky—they were decorated with yellow highlights and orange fruit, smeared with the scent of oak and syrup.

She stepped back to review her work.

It was a mess of color, of shifting wetness and dry pigment crusting over the edges, and she pursed her lips against the wave of dissatisfaction that roiled in her gut. There was something off, something that tugged at her like an anchor that longs for a taste of the black ocean.

It was all wrong.

A flash caught her eye.

The briefest speck of red glistened at the edge of the river, a stark contrast to the overlapping layers of brown paint it was buried in. She stepped closer, squinting skeptically down at the loose form. It must've been a stray hair on her brush, accidentally picking up the wrong pigments to form a poppy where poppies didn't belong.

Yes, that's what it was. A flower, merely out of place.

She scraped the speck from the canvas, wiped her stained brushes on a spare rag, and packed up her things.

"I really don't see it." Her sister cocked her head to the side with a frown. "It's just . . . a forest."

"That's not it, Sarah," She insisted. "The painting's all off."

"Do you think it needs a subject?"

"No, I mean . . ." She huffed. "Something about it just seems wrong."

"I don't think I'm following you." Sarah took a long drag of her cigarette, watching the smoke rise high above the balcony. The sun was sagging below the horizon, streaks of orange painted across the fading sky. "It honestly seems fine to me."

The two rested on Eleanor's balcony, sipping glasses of lemonade and watching the first shadows of night fall across the sky. The sisters hadn't seen each other in four months, with Sarah focusing on new endeavors in soapmaking (which was, unfortunately, just as dull as it sounded) and Eleanor pushing herself to release another string of original paintings.

"So, how have things been?" Her sister's voice was steady. Calm. "After . . . you know. Brian."

You know. She didn't have the courage to call it what it was—a murder.

"They still haven't found him," Eleanor replied. "His . . . body, I mean."

"It must've been hard, losing your husband so unexpectedly. And especially in that way."

That way. Eleanor's blood pounded in her head, and she knew from the doting look on her sister's face that the harsh lines were carved between her knit brows again, worn caverns appearing in seconds through skin. Sarah hated wrinkles, always kept her expressions tight and emotions clipped to avoid a single tear in her smooth, stark-white china face.

But Eleanor was the loose sister, the wild goose they kept locked away to avoid scaring the neighbors, or embarrassing the family, or attracting laughing, mocking boys in baseball caps and dirt-streaked navy shorts.

Being the family stain was hell, but at least she was allowed to have expressions.

"You're allowed to say murder, Sarah," She tried tiredly.

"I'm not made of glass, and I can certainly handle treating the situation as it is."

"Oh, Eleanor—"

"I haven't seen you in months, and it'll likely be more until we meet again. I don't want to spend the little time we have left talking about the murder."

Good riddance—the sister was quiet, and the two sat uncomfortably in silence once again.

Her eyes flitted back to the painting, lost in the folds of paint, of burnt sienna bark and titanium white clouds and the faintest traces of ochre in soft moss.

It should've been beautiful. It would've been beautiful, had it not been so wrong.

"Do you see that?"

Her sister raised a brow. "What, the painting again? You've made me review this thing about a dozen times today, and I've told you - there's nothing wrong with it."

But Eleanor was already creeping closer, a hand outstretched to caress the edges of the river, the canvas rough beneath her broken nails. There it was again—a stain of red in the water.

It wasn't just a speck this time - somehow, she'd overlooked a gaping scar that bled deep into the river.

"There's . . . there's red."

"What?"

"In the water."

Her sister sighed. "Why are you still going on about this? You and Father are the most stubborn perfectionists I've ever met, you hear?"

"I don't want to talk about Father, Sarah."

"He wasn't nearly as bad as you make him out to be." Eleanor let her fists curl but refused to swing them. What kind of sister was she, comparing Eleanor to him?

Nails dug bloody into palms. It occurred to her that she had been painting that day, too, when it happened.

Blood, blood, blood. Stains of red in the grass. Her tears in the dirt.

A fist, slamming over and over into her jaw.

Running, running, running—her dress hiked above ballet flats, his dark, hunched form chasing after her through the backyard. Both knew he'd catch her in seconds.

Blood, blood, blood.

Stains of red in the grass.

Eleanor swallowed. "You were always the favorite, weren't you? He never beat you for a reason."

"Don't be so dramatic, El," her sister scolded. "He hit you once or twice. It was never the end of the world."

Eleanor sighed. Tore her eyes from the painting, although the blood-red was never washed completely from where it tainted her mind. "You're right, I guess. It was never the end."

-

She slept on the couch that night, relinquishing the only bed to her sister. Even without the extra space, even with the cushions pressing painfully against her back, her legs hanging off the edge, it felt noticeably empty, as if someone had carved the beating heart of the room out with a blade.

It was his absence, she knew. His bellowing laughter, cheek pressed against the phone, a hand on her waist as she craned her neck to listen. His footsteps late at night, barking orders, fingers curling around the last milk carton in the house.

Somehow she still missed his touch, despite the bruises it left on her body. She missed the lingering eyes he marked her with the first time he'd seen her, as if painting a target on her forehead. She missed the messy scrawl of his handwriting, the unreadable scribbles on the first note he ever left her.

832-284-0000. Call me sometime.
-Brian

Was her grief a defect? Was she wrong to feel relieved that he was gone, yet still unhappy?

He was loud and clumsy and chaotic. Without him, the house was refined. Too quiet. Too clean.

And suddenly Eleanor was home again—not in the riverside cabin that she slept and worked in, but home, where the manor was never quiet with two little girls and a cat napping above the fireplace, soaking up the warmth of a hearth mid-October.

Father would be shouting at them to stop moving, stop screeching, stop playing, a cigar in his mouth as he eyed whatever documents were unlucky enough to be between his thick fingers that night. Sarah would obey, always. Eleanor would frown.

How could she still have affection for a place where her blood spilled on the dirt outside, where angry fists left bruises splattered over her eyes, and she'd have to sneak into Mother's closet the following morning to fish through whatever makeup could obscure them?

But the thought always lingered in her mind—was she expected to resent it instead, the home she'd been given? The place where her mother danced, her sister wrote notes over the spruce piano, her paintings hung over the walls?

The answer had been too hard to figure out. Maybe that's why she moved out into the backwoods, left the manor and the cat to Sarah. It was her home, but it was also her battlefield, and she'd been sick of fighting an endless war.

She just hadn't realized that she'd only return to the field years later with a different opponent.

Somewhere in the midst of her thoughts, her back had begun aching, spine grating against the stone-hard cushions, and she pulled herself sluggishly up onto her feet. It was too late in the night to be awake, but far too early to begin the day's work. She was a boat stranded between the end of one wind current, and the beginning of the next.

The world seemed static, empty, as she flitted through shifting shadows towards the kitchen. Silence gripped the room, begging to be interrupted by the churning of the coffee machine.

Her eyes slipped through the darkness again, flying back to the painting with magnetic energy as she waited for her coffee to pour. There was no doubt about it - the red stain in the river had grown again, this time seeping deep into the canvas and streaming through the water like poison.

She shuddered, gripped her mug until cold fingers turned white.

It was him. It had to be him.

Was she going insane? Had it finally happened, the years and the fists breaking through the delicate barrier of her mind? The house suddenly seemed emptier than she could've imagined, and Eleanor quickly reminded herself that Sarah was just above her, sleeping soundly in the bedroom upstairs.

He couldn't hurt her anymore. His fists were ash and dirt, his voice lost to the wind. But it felt as if he never left—none of them had. It was as if she fought one opponent in different forms, from father to husband, husband to spirit.

She'd have to act soon. That night—it had to be the last she saw of them.

-

"I'm heading out." Eleanor shoved a foot into her hiking boots, the painting wrapped in thick canvas and tucked under her armpit.

Sarah replied with only a grunt of acknowledgement, and with that, Eleanor closed the door behind her.

The walk through the forest was brief, the crisp Autumn air cutting into her cheeks like a blade. She remembered the first time she wandered down the now-familiar path that stretched before her.

Back when she was in the process of leaving the manor, the move to her cabin had been almost too rigid a change, switching from ballet flats to hiking boots, hardwood floors to moss carpets. But her desperation to leave her father's mansion had been just enough to keep her in place—a wide-eyed young woman, her thoughts solely focused on escape.

It was so long ago. Had she really come so far? Some days, she felt like the same Eleanor, the little girl who flinched at curled fists and hid behind her canvas.

She heard the soft gurgling of the river seconds before it came into view behind a heavyset grandfather oak tree. It looked the same as she'd left it that first day her brush touched the canvas, although red stains now soaked the latter like a plague.

From the knapsack against her hip she pulled a cardboard box of matches and a gallon of gasoline, tossing the ruined painting on the ground before her.

The canvas wrap slipped off of it, exposing the vivid green of the leaves, the birdsong, the smell of pine, as if she was peering into the scene itself - the day the water ahead of her first tasted blood.

Blood, blood, blood. Stains of red in the river. Her tears in the dirt.

A fist, slamming over and over into her jaw.

Running, running, running—her dress hiked above her boots, his dark, hunched form chasing after her through trees and bramble. Both knew he'd catch her in seconds.

The knife in her hand, lifting up. Her husband's cry of surprise. Blood, blood, blood.

Stains of red in the river.

She'd buried him where the red spot stretched over the painting, his knife tucked under his arm. Months later, young poppies were already spreading in droves over top, the body beneath forgotten by all but her.

The smell of gasoline lit her nostrils aflame as she opened the gallon tub and sprinkled liquid generously over the layers of paint she'd worked so hard to build, the world she'd captured in linseed oil and pigment.

The match was struck and dropped, and she waited with bated breath.

Flames turned to hellfire. The painting burned easily.

In the back of her mind, she imagined it as his cremation, his return to ashes and dirt and wind. It felt like an ending. It felt right.

She remembered the feeling of his arms around her, their sides pressed together, the taste of wine lingering on her lips as she leaned into his weight. She remembered his breath touching her lips, a gentle request to move closer.

She remembered the way he smiled, the way he laughed, the way he held her hand when she cried.

She remembered his quiet apologies in the morning, roses in hand, his fingers grazing over the bruises he'd left behind. She wondered if he loved her, after all that time. She wondered if, by some miracle, he'd been holding on because he'd missed a rose, missed one last apology, one last kiss, one last love letter dropped on her desk.

But his eyes had blazed before they'd gone out, slick-black with primitive, animal rage. She remembered his fists crushing her cheekbones, slamming into her stomach, and swallowed back her pity.

The painting curled in on itself, black and brown and mottled like rot.

And she knew that he was gone.

She wasn't sure if she believed in reincarnation, in an endless beginning and an unseeable end. But maybe one day, they'd meet again.

And she'd have her matches ready.

I KNOW THE CAGED BIRD

NIA SAMPSON

the first day of kindergarten, isla's brown paper bag skin rustles as if God is hyperventilating into her—sucking her in and out; she inflates and deflates as if there are no contents inside of her. she is creases and folds of brown skin.

isla doesn't know if she misses her mom. she is in an unfamiliar place and usually children ache for the familiarity of a mother in places like these, but she isn't certain if she'd be any better with her there. sometimes she had brown skin like isla inherited, lined with adipose in the places where isla used to be in her, hanging like wings from her arms.

sometimes, she was like last night.

isla had woken up to her parents fighting from somewhere in the house. she followed the noise to the kitchen—the back door cracked—where her dad had slipped out and a bird was ramming its head back and forth into the window, with tufts of its feathers falling into the sink. some instinct told isla to reach for it instead of closing the window. in her hands, its maw mauled and talons were crooked with bald patches some places on its belly. it scratched her cheek and flew up—somehow shapeshifting. isla blinked and her mother was lying face down on the floor, naked. "isla, honey," mrs. levine knocks on the restroom door. "is everything ok in there?"

isla nods to herself. yes, everything was fine.

she washes her hands, despite never actually doing anything and walks out. she slides back into her seat beside another black boy with girls' length curls.

196

"hi, do you—"

"*don't talk to me,*" isla warns.

the boy, whose name tag read "eli," obeyed as a bewildered dog would, "i don't want to . . . anymore."

no one talks to isla now, and it was best this way, she concluded. what if she became a bird, too? what if she became game?

*****

isla's mom stops smoking when she's in the second grade; says it isn't good for her lungs, as small as they are now. isla had determined she wanted to be an ornithologist at this point, an illogical attempt to cope with not understanding her mother.

her dad was on his way. he said he'd pick her up from school when he'd seen the fog this morning. isla asked if it was because birds didn't fly alone in the fog. he'd grabbed his hunting gun like a gas pump, by the trigger, and walked out.

eli sits beside her in the front where students wait for their parents to pick them up. he stared at the feathers on her coat, wanting to assume they came out of the places in it that had holes, despite the cotton that peeked out.

"my mom can take you home," he offers, trying hard not to look at her. "once she gets here."

isla stares at him: curls like the exposed spring in her mattress, lips soft in the place where he just lost his two front teeth. looking at him, she realizes an hour has passed.

yellow headlights flash in the white-gray. a vietnamese woman slips out of an SUV and runs up to him. "i'm *so sorry, eli.* i tried to get out of work, i tried—"

her dad had forgotten. he wasn't going to remember until he was sleeping in bed tonight with his gun, remembering her question to him, and then taking it into his dreams.

his mom's gaze tears away from the boy. "is this your friend?" eli shrugs. "can we bring her home, mom?"

maybe this is why her mom became a bird. to get the attention only a small animal could get. maybe her mom knew how much her dad liked hunting and was just trying, just trying to get his attention—the way he followed targets.

*****

in fourth grade, isla's dad brings back quail for dinner. he expects her mom to cook it. she huffs.

"isla, your friend, *eli,*" she clung to the name. "he invited you over for dinner, you can go—"

"*no,*" her dad commands. "we're going to eat together. don't you see the quail i got?"

don't you see the quail i got? he taunts. it deserves to be followed with a chuckle.

dinner smells so good, but isla's mouth snares shut. her mom stares at what she has done; her dad sucks the cartilage. it was like her mom would only breathe to remind herself that he was eating another thing instead of her.

the bird was cooked, but it was still dying.

her mother is still dying.

.

*****

"eli," isla whispers his name in the library.

he answers with his eyes, the way a deer does before you hit it in the middle of the street.

"when we were in kindergarten, do you remember what you were going to say to me?"

"when?"

"before i told you not to talk to me."

he's silent. they were laying on the floor, heads propped up against their backpacks, and his shirt was lifted so that she could see his skin stretching over his ribs.

"i'm sorry," she apologizes.

"*vô lý*," he says gently. "you were five, isla. that was eight years ago. i don't know why you remember that."

a moment passes and suddenly she feels his hand ghost over hers, hovering over it as if he is unsure if it's a booby trap. she does set ablaze when he finally touches her.

"i think i was going to ask if you wanted to be friends."

*****

freshman year, girls put chickens in isla's locker and laugh at her after her mother comes to school and literally caws at the principal in front of everyone for the first bullying incident.

eli tries to help her, calling her name, calling her *baby* in vietnamese, as the chickens peck her to death and hot tears fill her eyes: neck tight like having it held taut by a butcher on a cutting board: chest swelling with organs instead of air.

she runs. she runs. she runs. she hates that she can't just chew out the marrow from her bones like her dad and begin flying.

*****

when eli and isla are sixteen years old she goes to his house for the first time to eat congee for dinner. his mom pours steaming spoonfuls into their bowls.

"when are you all going to get married, already?" she jokes. she jokes. eli smiles.

"*chang bao lâu, me,*" he whispers.

she lets them take the SUV out and he brings her to a field somewhere. they open the trunk and sit in the back. a blasian boy and black girl in the back country. *chang bao lâu, me.* he kisses her and her heart hummingbirds, woodpeckers. there is no species for how wild it is, but it flies. it flies so fast, so high.

he lays her down and presses into her ribs with his thumbs and her insides spill out like yolk. she is sure she came first, the egg before the chicken. soon, mom. soon, mom. soon, mom.

isla wants to be an ornithologist to understand how the heart works.

*****

for black history month, isla's english class reads *i know why the caged bird sings* and is tested over it.

which line(s) from the poem show that the caged bird has never been free?

a. when her husband forced it to become prey (lines 9-10)
she places a question mark next to it.

b. when she set herself on fire to put out his hunger, which will
never be satisfied (line 48)

c. when she learns the cage itself is not what traps her (line 12)

201

d. when isla realized her mom was not bird, but fowl (line 114-115)

*****

"eli."

"yeah?"

"i got a perfect score on the maya angelou exam."

"were you questioning if you would?"

"i don't want you to see what's inside," she admits painfully as
they sit in her driveway, shame streaming down her face. "i'm
embarrassed of what's inside."

he looks at her hands. "what if you told me before i went inside?"
eli's mom had stitched her coat in the places where there had
been holes, but there were still feathers on her. she caught him
staring at them. she wasn't scared of becoming a bird. she wasn't
scared of him finding out that her mom was a bird. she was
scared of becoming her mother. not her mother as a bird, but
her mother as a human—who became what her dad called her
one night, who became less than because she was.

"are you really going to marry me, eli?" she asks, turning her head away from him. her throat felt like barbed wire. birds would be able to sit on it. there wasn't enough time.

"one day, i will, isla. *i'm* going to be the one to ask."

she gets out and stalks up to the screen door of the kitchen, eli running behind her. when they get inside, isla's dad is tilting his gun up at the ceiling where from it a shriek sounds. isla tears through the ripped screen door and rushes to where the feathers float to the ground, where the bird lay with two exit wounds through its sides.

"no! you'll shapeshift again!" isla blubbers as it twitches in her hands. "you'll become my mom again!"

the worms inside of her belly do not turn into intestines, her feathers do not stretch into skin, her beak does not collapse into mouth. she dies a bird. a species gone extinct.

eli kneels behind her and helps her pick up the feathers on the floor, sticking some inside her mother's wounds.

"i'm sorry," she says, pressing her cheek to her small chest. "that i let you back in that night. i'm so sorry. *i'm sorry.*"

it was never about her father. it was never about her father.

****

the night isla and eli marry, they release doves and consummate their relationship.

all the while of the consummation, isla thinks of her body as a site of entry and exit wounds which he may put there later. any place he touches has an aftertaste of insult to injury. when eli reaches out two fingers, they sink into her side instead of flying south—a migration of mourning.

Empty

Claire McNerney

After an hour alone in an empty classroom,
you start to feel heavy.
You can hear breathing that is not
quite matched up with your own,
An echo, a heartbeat
coming from the steady, silent walls.
Are the moving? Pulsing?
They're undulating, slowly, sickeningly transparent.
You can see the bones of the beast;
a ribcage beneath the paint and posters
of a monster that once was
beginning to be again.

A HALLOWEEN WISH

CORA LECATES

Oh, evil things!
In troves and swarms,
Let me join your vengeant storm!

I have but few and simple wishes:
Eerie candies and haunted dishes!
To greet a phantom as he passes,
And chatter with witches in my classes!

Hocus Pocus, ghastly ghouls!
Excite the chatter, invade the schools!
Enchant as a Pied Piper might—
But replace infectious tune with fright.

Oh, cover me in cobwebs, sweets!
I, too, want to flood the streets
Sneaky skeletons and things that crawl!
Allow me in your impish gall!

Ghosts in huddles,
Goblins in hordes,
You understand my wish, I'm sure.
Craft this October night of lore,
And end this autumn with chaos pure!

CONTRIBUTOR BIOS

MATHILDA BARR is a junior at Eagle Rock High School in Los Angeles, California. She has a deep-rooted passion for the outdoors, and a spark for travel. Her recent destinations have included treks across India, Mongolia, Santa Cruz Island, and more. She hopes to retain her love for nature, world culture, and exploration all throughout a life of adventure.

OLIVIA BELL is a high school senior from Chicago, Illinois. She is a recipient of the first place prize for poetry in the Arts Unlimited Community Art & Writing Contest, hosted by the *Daily Herald*, and an attendee of the Kenyon Young Writers Workshop, hosted through the *Kenyon Review*. In her free time, she works as the managing editor of her school's literary magazine, the *Free Run Press*.

PIA BHATIA is a junior from New Delhi, India. She currently writes and makes art for her school magazine and runs a website of her work: piabhatia.weebly.com. Her first collection, *Softshell*, is to be published soon.

MADDIE BOTTI is a junior from Boston, Massachusetts. She adores reading and writing and has an (unhealthy) obsession with Sylvia Plath and John Green. She is a fiction reader for *The Stirling Spoon*, an online literary magazine, and she recently attended the Iowa Young Writer's Studio. When she's not writing, she enjoys walking her dog, wandering into bookstores, and teaching swimming.

ANNA CARSON is a senior at the American International School in Israel. She hates math and loves reading, unless it's Shakespeare, and plans on becoming a journalist one day if she doesn't become a writer first.

ARTEMISIO ROMERO Y CARVER is sixteen-years old Chicano poet and visual artist. He spent three years in the Georgia O'Keeffe Boy's Program, and last summer attended Interlochen Arts Camp on scholarship. He has been published in *Rigorous Literary Journal* and *Inlandia Literary Journal* and was a finalist for the 2019 Santa Fe Youth Poet Laureate. He has performed original spoken word at the Lensic Performing Arts Center and Form & Concept Gallery. He once baked a cake that looked like Jeff Bezos.

Originally from Seattle, ANA CHEN is a freshman at Stanford University. Her writing has been recognized at international and national levels by the National Scholastic Art and Writing Awards, *The Adroit Journal, the Claremont Review, Polyphony Literary Magazine*, the New York Pitch Conference, and others. In 2019, she founded *It's Real* (itsrealmagazine.org), an online magazine seeking to destigmatize mental health issues in Asian American communities, followed by *Punderings*, a blog discussing art and activism, womanhood, college, and teenage angst. You can follow her on Instagram at @writerina.

ALAINA DISALVO is a sixteen-year-old, bisexual junior at Saint Saviour High School in Brooklyn, New York. She plans to study History and Sociology in college, with a concentration in Queer Studies. Later in life, Alaina hopes to become a professor in this field and make a difference in the lives of other queer kids. Her poem "Catholicism: A Student's Perspective" is available in the Winter 2019 edition of the *Rare Byrd Review*. She is a Ravenclaw with a love of reading, social activism, and Steven Universe.

JULIA DO is a high school writer from Orange County, California. She enjoys writing poetry, prose, and a combination of the two. She has participated in the *Kenyon Review* Young Writers Workshop and has had her work published in its anthology and in *Creative Communication*.

ANUSHKA E. is a fourteen-year-old high school freshmen from New Jersey. From a young age, she has harbored an endless passion for writing, especially poetry. As a dog lover, travel enthusiast, and Netflix addict, Anushka continuously searches for outlets to explore her interests. She believes poetry is her greatest form of expression and is always creating stories through her words.

MARGAUX EMMANUEL is a sixteen-year-old French-American student at the French high school in Kita-ku, Tokyo. She is a student in the literature and language section at her school by day, a kickboxer in the evenings, and a writer by night. She has been book blogging for about four years (https://theyoungreadersreview.blogspot.com) and frequently participates in spoken word events in Tokyo.

MAYA EPSTEIN is a sophomore with a pen from Aurora, Colorado. When she isn't writing and drinking inordinate amounts of coffee, she loves practicing yoga, thrifting, and drinking inordinate amounts of tea. Empathy is her superpower, and she's still waiting for the day Edna Mode designs her a super-suit. She hopes you have the most wonderful day!

ALI FISHMAN is a sophomore living in San Francisco, CA. She attends San Francisco University High School. She plays volleyball, basketball, and softball. In addition to sports she enjoys photography, surfing, and binge watching Netflix. Her favorite show is *How I Met Your Mother*. She lives with her sister, mother, father, and brother.

LUCIA MARGARITA FOLLMAN is a high school junior in San Antonio, Texas. In addition to writing fiction, She enjoys painting, travelling, and looking for adventure.

JIMMY FRANCIS is an actor/comedian/impressionist/writer/musician/songwriter/poet and amateur historian. His head is full of worthless information. He wrote, produced, and directed a short film for MTV's AIDS Awareness Project. He made a graphic novel, *Hyperdork: Years And Years Of Trauma*, based on his stand-up comedy act (available on Amazon) which has received positive reviews from *Fanboy Comics* and *Slurred Nerd*. He won a stand-up competition at Flappers Comedy Club in Burbank, California, and a best actor award from the Inland Theatre League for playing Billy Bibbit in the play "One Flew Over The Cuckoo's Nest."

ANNA FRANKL is a seventeen-year-old high school student living in Seoul, South Korea. She has won an honorable mention for the Scholastic Art and Writing awards. She has been drawing since the age of three, and has ever since remained adamant in her wish of becoming a professional artist. Artist tumblr: dr-chalk.tumblr.com

SLOKA GANNE is thirteen-years-old and loves sketching.

LITA GI is an upcoming junior in Pennsylvania who enjoys reading classical literature. She prefers to write stories that allow her characters to thrive, and she listens to artists such as Roo Panes and Gotye for inspiration. She has received the Certificate of Achievement of Excellence in English in both seventh and ninth grade, along with smaller class-wide awards for writing. When she's procrastinating on her work, you can find her drawing, spending quality time/bickering with her siblings, and talking to her potted plants. She loves Brazilian food, old libraries, collecting vinyl, and obsessively fawning over fictional characters.

SABRINA GUO is a Syosset High School freshman from Oyster Bay, New York. She is a recipient of the Civic Expression Award, three National Gold Medals in Poetry, and a National Gold Medal in Journalism from the Scholastic Art & Writing Awards. Her work has also been recognized by the Academy of American Poets, the Sarah Mook Poetry Contest, the 1455 Teen Poet Contest, the *Stone Soup* Concrete Poetry Contest, and the *Stone Soup* Flash Fiction Contest. Her recent work is featured in the *Best Teen Writing* of 2019, the Alliance for Young Artists & Writers blog, and *Stone Soup*.

DEDEEPYA GUTHIKONDA is a fifteen-year-old high school student from Edina, Minnesota. You can find her at any time reading, writing and occasionally binging Netflix (don't worry, it's for inspiration). This past summer she attended the Summer Writing Residency at the University of Iowa.

ANNE GVOZDJAK is a sophomore at Bellevue High School in Seattle, Washington. Besides writing poetry and working on her novel, she likes spending her time by listening to music, exploring graphic design, doing calligraphy, and reading.

SOPHIA HLAVATY is a high school junior at Phillips Academy aspiring to study political science. Her work has been featured and/or recognized by the Scholastic Art and Writing Awards, *The Apprentice Writer, Blue Marble Review*, and various school publications.

RUSUDAN JANJALASHVILI is an eigtheen-year-old student from Tbilisi, Georgia, who prefers to be called Rusa. She has successfully graduated from the public school N.63 and now specializes in law in Tbilisi State University. Love for literature and the passion of writing have been her hobbies since childhood. She loves reading Gothic literature and creating one as well. Poe and Lovecraft are her favorite writers, who have had a great influence on her to write both prose and poetry. She is already a published writer—her work "My Ancestor in My Age" was published in the youth literature almanac by *SOVLAB* in 2018. She also loves writing articles. She was offered to be the author of the History Campus Blog based in Hamburg, Germany and her article "Love for Writing Runs in My Blood" was chosen to be published on the blog.

KEVIN KONG is a junior at A.W. Dreyfoos School of the Arts in Florida. His writing has been recognized by the Florida State Poets Association and the Scholastic Art & Writing Awards. His poetry has been published in *Teen Ink* and *Bridge Ink* and is forthcoming in the FSPA anthology, *Cadence*. He enjoys playing the cello and eating hotpot.

GIANA LASPINA is a sophomore attending Joun Overton High School in Nashville, TN. She has been accepted to the Teens Take the Frist contest at the Frist Museum. She is a proud vegan, and an avid artist and writer, and has a strong love for coffee. When she isn't drawing, you can find her playing bass, or listening to punk music.

R.M. LAWLER is a high school senior from eastern Kansas with a fierce love of words and Trivial Pursuit. Besides writing, she also enjoys being outdoors, reading, and volunteering. In her free time, you can probably find her enjoying either Buzzfeed Unsolved or a classic '90s rom-com.

CORA LECATES attends Saint Ann's School in Brooklyn, New York. She is fifteen and entering tenth grade and enjoys reading and writing of all kinds. She is previously unpublished.

HYUNG JIN (ERIKA) LEE is a senior at the Hun School of Princeton in New Jersey. Her work was recognized at the national level through the Scholastic Art and Writing Awards, awarded first place at the FAA High School Competition, and published in various publications such as the *Balloon Lit, CrashTest,* and *Celebrating Art.* The way that fine art can capture a fragment of time like no other medium inspires her and drives her to continue painting and drawing.
Artist Instagram: https://www.instagram.com/erikalee_art/
Personal art website: https://hyunglee.wixsite.com/mysite-3

SYDNEY LEE is a current rising senior at YCIS in Beijing, China. Her artwork has been published on the cover of *InkBeat Literary Magazine* and has received Honorable Mention in the Discover FAA International High School Art and Design competition. She was a finalist in the Lowell Milken Center ArtEffect competition and the IIX She Is More Youth Art Competition. Her work has been included in an IIX art exhibition and has also been exhibited at M WOODS Museum alongside the work of Richard Tuttle. When not writing or reading, she can be caught painting or knitting furiously.

ALIZA LI is a seventeen-year-old attending Stephen F. Austin High School in Sugar Land, Texas. She is a whopping four-feet-eleven-inches of pure creative energy and enjoys staying up late and watching Buzzfeed Unsolved. Aliza has published work in *Aerie International* student literary journal and has a received a silver key in the Scholastic Art & Writing awards. She hopes to one day become a published author and share with the world the same magic that entranced her to write when she was young.

NICOLE LI is a rising high school senior at Shanghai American School in Shanghai, China. Her writing has been recognized by the National Scholastic Art & Writing Awards and the *New York Times,* and can be found in the *Eunoia Review* and *Polyphony Lit,* among others. She enjoys making lists, discovering new podcasts, and petting other people's cats. She hopes magic finds you today.

TIFFANY LIU is a high school senior from Long Island, New York looking to pursue marketing. She is the winner of the Superior Writing Award for the 2019 NCTE Writing Competition. If she's not reading or writing, she can be found rowing for her school team, jamming out to classic rock, or traveling to a faraway place on the other side of the world.

A junior in Waterloo, Ontario, MICHELLE MA is a proud Canadian. She loves baking and writing, and has been doggedly trying to get back into reading actual, paper books. Despite her chronic case of overambition and a Planck-length attention span, when it comes to stories, she always finishes what she starts.

JENNIFER MARTOCCI is a sophomore at Fleming Island High School in Florida. She is an active participant in the writing club at her high school and enjoys writing short stories and poetry. She is glad to have her family and friends, as well as her six mischievous chickens, to support her in her passion to write. She thanks the *Canvas Literary Journal* for accepting and perusing her entry.

CLAIRE MCNERNEY is a junior from Pleasanton, California. When not writing, she can be found performing onstage or listening to audio dramas. She recently started an anthology podcast, *Cumulonimbus*, which can be found on all good podcasting platforms.

JODIE MENG is a rising senior ('20) at the Illinois Math and Science Academy in Aurora, Illinois. She enjoys writing for her school newspaper, researching, and volunteering around the community. Her writing is forthcoming in the *Chautauqua Literary Journal*.

OREO_M is a fourteen-year-old girl from Gauteng, South Africa. As a high school student from Hoerskool Akasia she enjoys all types of art, which allow her to express herself and give the world or fellow scholars a view of things from her perspective. She enjoys spending her free time writing both poems and songs and reading short stories. Oreo_M loves dancing, singing, cooking, baking, and drawing. She is not only one artistic young girl but is a smart young lady with big dreams and ambitions of changing the world through her art.

DRISHIKA NADELLA is a student of science from India. She has been previously published in *GERM Magazine*, *Stepping Stones*, *Sprout*, *Quail Bell*, and elsewhere.

JYOTSNA NAIR is a fifteen-year-old living in India (as well as her own imagination). She enjoys baking banana bread and consuming it over books.

NOAH OH lives in Scarsdale, New York. He is thirteen and going into eighth grade. He goes to school at Edgemont Junior-Senior High School and enjoys playing soccer and writing.

NATALIE OWEN is a seventeen-year-old high school senior from Boston, Massachusetts. She loves to read Joan Didion and Vladimir Nabokov, among many other authors, and she writes as a form of catharsis, creation, and thought condensation.

GRACE PENG was raised in Dallas, Texas. She is sixteen. When she is not busy writing, she is reading poetry, taking photos, enjoying food, and traveling.

SOFIA PHAM is a junior at Seven Lakes High School in Katy, Texas. She is currently Vice President of Women Inspiring Social Harmony, a workshop dedicated to educating young girls in writing, STEM, and leadership. An avid reader and writer, Sofia also serves as an advertising manager for the Seven Lakes school magazine, *The Torch*. She enjoys making art, playing piano, and ravenously consuming bubble tea.

LAYA REDDY is a rising junior at Adlai E. Stevenson High School in Lincolnshire, Illinois. She has been recognized by the National Scholastic Arts & Writing Awards, and other works of her are forthcoming in *Hypernova Lit Magazine*. She enjoys munching on bell peppers and devouring Sylvia Plath's poetry.

NIA SAMPSON is a sixteen-year-old who lives in Houston, Texas. She has previously been awarded the Silver Key for the Scholastic Art and Writing Awards for her work. She enjoys dreaming of things that may never be.

PRIYANKA SHRESTHA lives in Cleveland, Ohio and will be a senior at Beachwood High School. She has previously won numerous Scholastic Art and Writing Awards, including three Gold Keys, two Silver Keys, and five honorable mentions. Though she spends more time thinking about what she's going to write than actually getting to writing it, Priyanka enjoys writing mostly short stories and poetry. If she's not writing or daydreaming she can be found practicing Karate, playing the piano, or spending time with her family. Her hidden talent is being a master of all types of DIY braids and hairstyles.

MAIA SIEGEL's poetry has appeared in *Polyphony Lit*, *Cargoes*, the AIPF (Austin International Poetry Festival) Youth Anthology, *The Claremont Review,* and elsewhere. She has been recognized by The Poetry Society and The Scholastic Art & Writing Awards.

She will attend Interlochen Arts Academy in the fall, after winning their Virginia B. Ball scholarship.

SARAH UHLMAN is an only slightly rebellious teen who mostly writes at ungodly hours of the night in her room. she loves bad horror movies, good poetry, and beautiful strangers.

CYNTHIA WANG is a seventeen-year-old high school senior at Shanghai American School Pudong from Shanghai, China. A self-declared bookworm and diagnosed philosophy addict, Cynthia spends her free time writing for her blog Quotidian Musings. Otherwise, one would find her blinking away her lack of sleep—a common characteristic found in fellow IB diploma victims. Above all, she hopes that one day, she could break through her culture of silence—that one day, through her words, her voice might be heard.

PATRICK WANG is a rising senior at Northview High School. He is an avid writer and artist always dedicated to searching out new voices. He has attended the *Kenyon Review* Young Writers workshop, been published by the American High School Poets, and excerpted in the *New York Times*. He is an avid defender of minority voices and his favorite television shows.

CATHLEEN WENG is a high school senior from South Dakota. She has been awarded with a regional gold key in the Scholastic Arts & Writing Competition and an honorable mention in the Leonard L. Milberg Poetry Contest. Aside from writing, she reluctantly plays the violin and avidly consumes fantasy novels.

ANNA WENZEL is a tenth grader in Colorado. She has been published in the local paper, the *Boulder Weekly*. She loves reading, writing, and building LEGO sculptures. Her favorite authors are V.E. Schwab and Sarah J Maas.

ALEXIS YANG is a seventeen-year-old at Smithtown High School East in Saint James, New York. She has received a national gold medal and several regional awards from the Scholastic Art & Writing Awards for fiction. When she isn't writing, she enjoys playing the guitar and eating copious amounts of blueberries.

About Canvas

est. 2013

Canvas Teen Literary Journal publishes the work of teen writers and artists 13-18 years old, read and rated by a board of teen editors. Our contributors and editors are from all over the English-speaking world and represent some of the best teen writing out there, in our humble opinion.

Canvas was established by Writers & Books in Rochester, New York in 2013, ran continuously for 4 years, took a 1.5 year hiatus, and was restructured and re-established by Cosmographia Books in 2018. Nina Alvarez and Lindsay Herko both oversee the publication of the journal.

Each issue is available to read for free at CanvasLiteraryJournal.com. Issues are available through amazon and at a growing number of libraries.